ADULTS GUIDE

TO

BETTER SWIMMING

Katie Smith

Adults Guide To Better Swimming

Illustrations by Emma Wright

Also available as an e-book.

Contact: katieswimguides@yahoo.com.au

ISBN-10: 099243632X
ISBN-13: 978-0-9924363-2-2

CONTENTS

GETTING STARTED

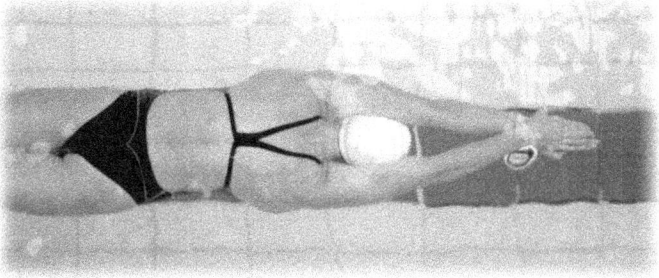

- ✪ I Want To Swim
- ✪ Time Required
- ✪ Equipment

INTRODUCTION

Welcome to the **Adults Guide To Better Swimming**! I'm guessing you are one of the many adults out there who has, at some stage, learnt how to swim – but is not particularly proficient at it. While you may be able to save yourself if you fell into deep water, you probably can't swim very many laps of a 50 metre pool. Don't worry, you're not alone. In fact you're in the majority. While most Australian adults have had exposure to water and those up to their fifties have probably taken part in a school swimming program of some kind, not that many have a technically correct freestyle stroke and very few can swim more than about 100 metres in one go.

If you have purchased this book, I'm assuming that you would like to improve your swimming skills. Good on you! Swimming is a great sport that provides many health benefits. But more than that it's relaxing and a lot of fun. It is also a sport that you can take very easily and gently or you can ramp up a few notches and have a great workout. The best thing is that it is never too late to work on your swimming skills.

Don't worry if you haven't been in a pool in years, or if you never learnt to breathe properly or if your kick is lacklustre. These are all things we can work on. I am assuming you have at least basic swimming skills – you can put your face under the water, float and kick and can attempt a basic freestyle stroke. If you have never been in the water before, this guide will be too advanced for you. (If you are scared to put your head under the water you might want to try my other book *Learning To Swim When You're Scared: How To Overcome a Fear of Water.* Its main focus is on learning to submerge.)

To be completely honest the best way to improve your swimming skills is to take part in a stroke correction class with a trained swimming teacher. Nothing can match that kind of instruction. However not everybody is able to access swimming classes. Maybe your local pool doesn't offer them for adults. Maybe the times such classes are offered are not convenient for you. Perhaps you can't afford it or you're simply embarrassed because you're fifty years old and have never learnt how to swim properly. In any of those cases (or for any other reason) this book is the next best thing. It will take your through the basics as well as point out the most common issues adults struggle with when learning how to swim properly. It's not a magic fix and you will have to work at it, but the rewards will be very worthwhile.

I WANT TO SWIM!

Picture this scenario. Summer is coming around and you're looking for an exercise to do that will get you fit and healthy as well as lose a few kilos. You're not much of a runner, hate the gym and you had to give up tennis after you hurt your knee. You drive past the local pool on your way to and from work every day and whenever you look in there you see people in the water doing laps. I should do that, you tell yourself. I learnt how to swim when I was a kid and while I haven't been in the water for a while it's like riding a bike, right? Now the weather is getting warmer it would be a great thing to do in the morning before work.

So, you get organised. You buy yourself some new swimmers, invest in a cap and goggles and dig out your old beach towel. Arriving at the pool one morning you're amazed at just how many people are in there swimming laps and the best news is that they're not all young and super fit. There are lots of older people taking things at a nice, leisurely pace. I'll start off slow, you think to yourself. I'll just do ten laps today, surely I can manage that. You climb down into the cool water and immediately feel relaxed and ready to go. Ducking under the water you push off the wall and start stoking. See, you tell yourself, it really is like riding a bike, you haven't forgotten how to swim after all! The first few strokes feel great. You're feeling comfortable in the water and you're managing to stay on your side of the lane. This continues for a little while longer but then things start to fall apart. Each time you turn to breathe you feel like you need to suck more air in. You start breathing every third stroke, then every second but it's still not enough. Now your arms are starting to hurt a bit and your legs feel heavy. The kick you started with has petered down to an occasional feeble leg movement. Worst of all you're getting a stitch.

The end, you think to yourself, I just have to make it to the end! Desperately you push on, each stroke taking more energy and each breath becoming more of a gulp than the one before. Out of the corner of your eye you notice the ladder. But it's not the ladder at the deep end, it's the one in the middle of the pool. You've only swum 25 metres and you're dying! Too embarrassed to just stop, you switch to a feeble breaststroke. At least it keeps your head out of the water, but it hurts almost as much. When you finally make it to the other end you have to cling to the lane rope to try and catch your breath as the other swimmers move past you effortlessly. Disheartened, but not beaten, you rest a bit and then attempt another lap. Maybe this time it won't be so bad, you hope. But unfortunately, it's worse and this time you do have to stop. Embarrassed at your lack of fitness, you slink out of the pool and decide that swimming is just not for you after all.

Unfortunately, this is the point at which most adults give up. Realising that swimming is not quite as easy as it looks, they think they'll never be able to improve their skills to the point where they'll be able to complete a proper workout in the water. It's such a shame, because with some work and determination just about anybody can become a proficient swimmer. It will take time and it will take effort – but like any new skill with enough practice you will soon start to see rapid improvement.

As you work through this guide, remind yourself frequently that Rome wasn't built in a day. Don't get discouraged if your first few sessions seem to produce very little result. Give yourself at least six weeks (averaging around three or four sessions a week) to really get your water lungs and several months after that to build up to some distance.

Swimming is no different to any other physical activity, it requires consistent practice over an extended time period to improve. Remember too that you will have to take your stroke apart to some degree and rebuild it. Breaking decades of old habits is not easy and will require focus and effort for a time. But the strands will all come together eventually and the frustration of the start of the process will be forgotten.

This book is about your swimming journey so you should set your own goals and work towards them in a way that makes sense to you. Keep a diary of what you accomplish each week. And if, heaven forbid, you fall off the wagon and have a week or two off, don't give up all together. Muscle memory is a wonderful thing and even if your fitness slips back a little, you will never revert right back to where you started.

EQUIPMENT NEEDED

Fortunately swimming is a sport that doesn't require a lot of expensive equipment. There are a few basics that I recommend, but it is entirely up to you what you whether or not you get them.

Obviously the first thing you want is a good quality swimsuit. I strongly suggest getting a chlorine resistant fabric. While it may be more expensive than Lycra, it will last five or even ten times as long. All the major brands have chlorine resistant ranges. While sun safety is important, it is much easier to swim without being weighed down by rash vests, t-shirts or long board shorts. They really do increase the drag in the water and will have an impact on the way you swim. Perhaps you could use an indoor pool or choose a time when the sun is not too strong. For women just a plain one piece is perfect, or if you choose two piece make sure it's a sporty two piece rather than a bikini or tankini. You want to concentrate on your swimming, not on what your swimwear is doing! For men either the Speedo style briefs or the knee length trunks are best. Long board shorts will act like a parachute as you swim. Like the women, you want to concentrate on your swimming not be annoyed about your boardies billowing around you. If you are body conscious choose a style that covers well (for example you can get women's swimwear with built in legs and/or high neck and back). Remember too that once you are in the water and moving nobody will pay any attention to what you are wearing.

A swimming cap is also a very good idea for women (unless you have very short hair). Not only does it keep your hair out of your face, it will also help protect your locks from at least some of the ravages of chlorine. A cap also makes it much easier to put your goggles on and off. (In addition, if you wear goggles without a cap, your hair will get a lot of breakage along the goggle line. Ask any hairdresser if you don't believe me!). Men can also wear a cap if they choose but because their hair is generally shorter (or non-existent in some cases), it's not a necessity. The best kind of swimming cap to get is a silicone one as it will last years with proper care and is the easiest to get on and off. While they are the most expensive up front (although still relatively cheap), a silicone cap will easily outlast any other kind. A lycra/cloth cap is kinder to your hair and will have a fair life span but with continued use the elastic and fabric will degrade and become stretched and loose. A latex cap is the cheapest and the least user friendly. Latex caps tend to be harder to put on, are tighter around the edge (sometimes uncomfortably so) and rip easily. They also tend to deteriorate when stored for any length of time. Having said all that though the choice is ultimately yours. Swimming caps tend to be one size, but some brands do offer a larger size which is best for women with long hair who need to put it up under the cap. There is a bit of a learning curve when putting your swimming cap on, but you soon get the hang of it. With proper care (rinse and dry after use) a quality swimming cap should last for several years.

Goggles are a necessity if you want to do any kind of swimming training. Not only will they protect your eyes from the harshness of the chlorine in the pool, they will also give you much, much better visibility in the water. If you have never worn goggles, try a pair and notice the massive difference in what you can see underwater. Again, be prepared to pay a bit more for a quality pair, rather than be lured by cheap brands. Anything over $20 should get you a good set. Ask at your local pool or sports store for the most popular brands. You can't go too far wrong on brands like Speedo, Zoggs or Vorgee. Goggles can have clear, tinted or mirrored lenses, which one you choose is personal preference. If you swim indoors, there is no real need for tinted lenses, for example. Some brands also have male and female versions, this will also come down to personal preference. Follow the manufacturer's directions to get the best result from your goggles. You can also get prescription goggles if your eyesight is not the best.

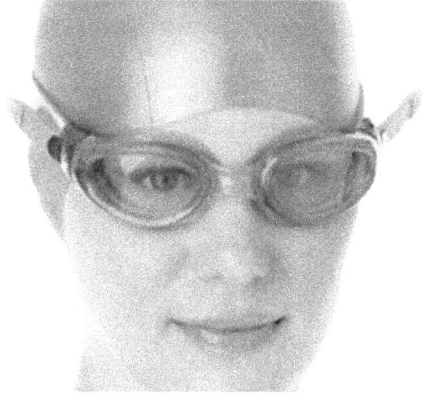

Note: a good way to keep your goggles from fogging up is to smear a drop of baby shampoo into each lens then rinse thoroughly. (You shouldn't see any residue). Ideally rinse in fresh water but using chlorinated or salt water works fine as well. Rinsing your goggles after use is recommended too. You can also use an anti-fogging spray/stick which also effective but will cost you more. I have found that even the most expensive goggles will fog up after a certain period of time. Taking measures to prevent fogging before you swim will prevent a lot of frustration and the need to remove and rinse your goggles while swimming.

You may also like to get a kickboard and a pull buoy. Check first at your local pool, though, as many will offer equipment for hire or free loan. If you decide to purchase your own none of these things are particularly expensive. They are available at department stores like Big W and K-Mart, at sports stores like Rebel Sport or Super A-Mart, at public pools and on-line.

Kickboard

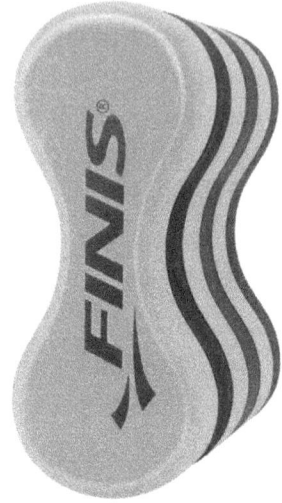

Pull Buoy

If you do buy your own equipment, you should also get a mesh style bag to carry it all in. All the major brands have these equipment bags. The mesh allows the equipment to dry properly, preventing mould and mildew forming on it. It is also much easier keeping all your gear together. It is smart to keep your swimming bag in the boot of your car, thus alleviating the need to put things in and out every time you go to the pool. There is nothing more annoying than arriving to train and realising you've left something at home.

You should clearly label your own things in permanent marker so you can easily prove ownership should your equipment get mixed up or misplaced at the pool.

USE OF FINS/FLIPPERS

The use of fins/flippers is a great tool in improving your swimming skills. Not only do they provide extra buoyancy, they also provide extra power in your kick, allowing you to swim faster and with less effort. For those who have struggled with swimming any kind of distance, the first time you swim with fins on can feel magic. The caveat, however, is that they have to be used sparingly. If you become overly reliant on fins, you will find it very difficult to transition back to swimming without them. Fins are best used during warm up to allow you to relax and ease into your swim, during drills to provide buoyancy and during warm down, once again to allow you to relax when fatigued. They can also be used occasionally during a speed set or something similar. I will talk about fins/flippers several times throughout this book.

There are two different types of fins, standard (or floating) fins and short fins. Standard fins have a long blade that floats easily on the surface of the water and lifts the hips and legs high. They are generally made of rubber and due to their increased surface area, provide great power in the kick, but only provide resistance on the down kick, thus not working the up kick. It is also impossible to kick at a high tempo with long fins. Short fins, such as the DMC brand, are generally made of silicone and are worn looser on the foot. (Some brands do have the normal enclosed food pouch). The shorter blade still provides buoyancy and generates extra power in the kick, but it works both the up and down kick, thus working the legs more consistently and producing a more natural and faster kicking style.

If you are used to standard fins, the shorter fins will feel heavier and less powerful to begin with, but you soon adjust to the different feel of them. I recommend short fins over standard, however if you only have standard, they are adequate for the average recreational swimmer. Standard fins are most suitable for beginners who struggle to keep their legs on the surface.

The most important thing with your fins is that they fit correctly. Standard fins will generally have an enclosed foot pouch and your foot should fit snugly within it. If they are too tight, they will cause blisters on your toes. If they are too big, the sliding motion will decrease their effectiveness and they may also fall off. Shorter fins usually have an ankle strap and a looser fit. Check their fit guide to make sure you have the right size for your foot, especially if you have been used to standard fins.

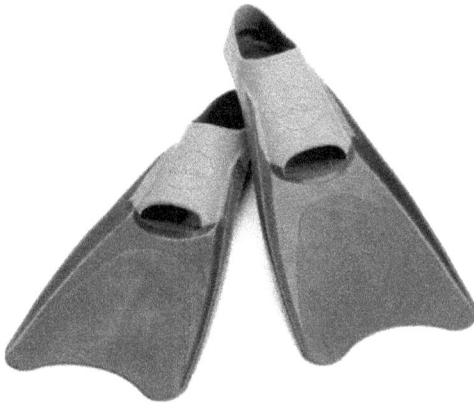

Standard Floating Fins

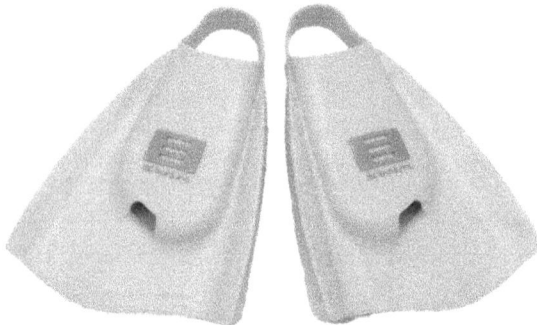

Short Fins

TIME COMMITMENT

So, how often do you need to swim to make good progress? Ideally, in the beginning if you can swim four times per week (even if only for the first few weeks), you will build a great, strong foundation for your swimming skills. Ultimately, though any amount of time you put in will be beneficial – but in simple terms the more you do the better. The early sessions don't have to be long – in fact I would recommend shorter sessions to begin with. Half an hour is great – gradually building to an hour if possible. If you are using a public pool, check if they have weekly or monthly passes to make it more economical. To see consistent improvement, you should aim for a minimum of two sessions per week, although three or more will produce faster results. That third session seems to be where the magic happens. This book is not about short cuts to swimming success because sadly there are none, it is time and targeted effort that will produce results.

Also, ask the pool staff when the quietest times are. Almost all public pools have swimming lessons for children as well as squad, aqua aerobics, water polo and other activities. When you're just starting out, you should aim to go at a time when there is a lot of lane space and you can work at your own pace without having to rush or feel like you're being scrutinised by other swimmers. Weekdays during school hours are often good or perhaps early in the morning or later in the evening. Pools often provide a timetable of activities so you can plan your swimming around that. Remember, too, that some pools are busier than others. While a longer drive to a quieter pool can seem inconvenient, if you get your own lane and set your own pace it is probably worth the effort.

Note: You don't have to use a public pool to work on your swimming skills. If you have access to a private pool, that is fine for the early stages. You will probably want to transition to a larger pool (at least 25 metres) when you start to work on distance, but this can be occasional while continuing to practice in a smaller pool.

What Do I Gain?

For the purposes of this swimming guide, I am going to concentrate mainly on building your skills and distance in freestyle. Why? Because it is the stroke most commonly used in distance swimming workouts. It is also the stroke that most people can manage to at least a basic level. I have included some basic information about backstroke and breaststroke towards the end of the manual, but I have not covered butterfly.

This manual is designed for people who are looking to build on their existing swimming skills to the point where they are able to complete a distance workout (between one and two kilometres). It is focused on technique and building a good foundation for your freestyle stroke but does not cover racing or advanced coaching advice. If that is what you are seeking you may need to look to a more technical guide.

I have broken the swimming process down into a number of steps. The idea is for you to work on each step and become proficient before moving onto the next. How long each step takes will vary for each individual. You may already be proficient at some aspects and can move quickly onto the next skill. Or you may be prepared to get in the pool every day and practice, which will also move you through the steps faster. Resist the urge to skip ahead without covering each skill. There is a method in my progression that is designed to get you strong in the basics first before tackling technique.

I have used only metric distances (metres); however for pool lengths the variation between metres and yards is not too significant. 50 metres is the length of an Olympic sized pool (with 25 metres obviously half that length). A 50/25 yard pool will be slightly shorter or to look at it the other way a 50 metre pool is approximately 54 yards, a 25 metre is 27 yards. Many 50 metre pools have a ladder positioned at halfway as an easy reference point if you are looking to swim shorter distances to start with. Most ten lane 50 metre pools are actually 25 metres wide and will sometimes configure their lanes sideways to maximise lane space.

HEATED VS NON-HEATED POOL

Whether you choose to swim in heated or non-heated pool largely comes down to personal preference and climatic conditions. Unless you live in a very hot climate almost all outdoor pools will be heated in the cooler months. Outdoor pools will generally seem cooler than indoor (even if the water temperature is the same). There are a couple of reasons for this. Most obviously is that outdoor pools are affected by air temperature, wind and rain and also the steam from the heated water is quickly dissipated. Indoor pools can control their air temperature (either through air-conditioning or heating) and this has a big impact on how the water feels.

The over-riding factor you want to take into consideration is personal comfort. Different people tolerate water temperatures in different ways. Growing up in a warm climate I'm a sook when it comes to cold water, but those from cooler climates think nothing of diving into pools that give me goose bumps. It will often seem cold when you first get in, but you should warm up after swimming a few laps. If you are still shivering after this then the pool is probably too cold. Your body is affected by extremes in temperature and you will be more prone to cramps if your core temperature is lower than normal. You will also not swim your best if your body is diverting all its energy towards trying to keep yourself warm.

A comfortable temperature for swimming in a heated pool is around 27/28 degrees Celsius (80 degrees Fahrenheit). In winter this can seem cold to the touch initially, but once you get in and moving you will warm up. It can be tempting to choose a warmer indoor pool (some are as warm as 32 degrees Celsius/90 Fahrenheit) but this can become quite uncomfortable once you get moving (kind of like running when it's very humid). The staff should be able to tell you the water temperature of any/all pools in the complex.

Make use of heated pools in the colder months (or all year if you live in a cold climate) – you don't want to lose all the momentum and fitness you have built up by having a six to eight month break. Pools are also much quieter in the winter, providing you with a wider choice in times and lane space. Besides that, there is nothing quite like a nice hot shower and a warm drink after your swim.

Keeping warm before and after you swim is also a major consideration with winter swimming. Rug up as much as you need to until the moment you have to get in the water. This may include a beanie and ugg boots, as keeping your head and feet warm is important. A swimming/deck coat is ideal for winter swimming. Designed to be worn before and after your swim (even when wet), it allows you to stay warm without having to dress in layers of clothes. Getting in the water is the hardest part, once in and warmed up you will be reluctant to get out again.

Despite the chill factor, there is something exhilarating about winter swimming, especially in an outdoor pool. The welcome plume of steam rising above the water really is very inviting! Once you get past the mental block of swimming when the air temperature is cold, you will realise what a waste it is to take time off over winter.

Tip: Although the idea of swimming early in the morning in winter may seem uninviting, it is the time when the water is generally the warmest, believe it or not. Heated pools are covered overnight and when the covers are lifted off the top layer of the water (where the cover has stopped the steam escaping) is the warmest. The other bonus is you will almost certainly get a lane to yourself.

SKILL BUILDING

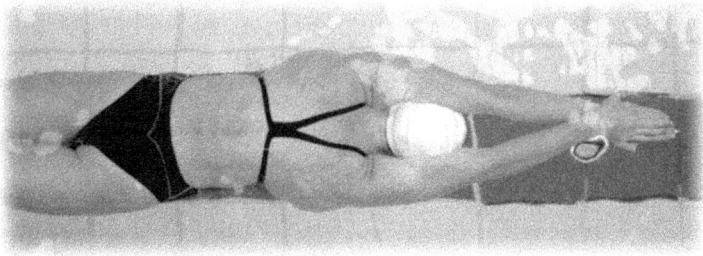

- ✪ Bubbles
- ✪ Breathing
- ✪ Body Position

PRACTICE, PRACTICE, PRACTICE
(BUT GET IT RIGHT FIRST)

It can be tempting to just get in the pool and swim lap after lap, with the idea that the further you swim the more you will improve. While you may get fitter by doing this, if your technique is incorrect all you are doing is reinforcing bad habits. If your body position is not right or you don't know how to breathe properly, doing endless laps will not magically improve either of those things.

With each of the skills I have outlined, you need to get them right and practice them a lot before you move onto the next part. As mentioned before, you may already be proficient at some skills and can move on quickly, but you still need to check each one as you go. (Chances are if you are reading this book you will need to work on most of the skills outlined in the coming chapter).

I deliberately use short distances to start with so you can incorporate each skill into your freestyle stroke without getting too tired. Remember your brain already has entrenched neural pathways where your previous swimming habits reside. The great news is that you can build new pathways, but the old pathways will remain and will revisit as soon as you let them. If you take the time to practice a new skill a dozen times over a manageable short distance you will train your brain to keep that skill up. If you decide you will just swim 400 metres nonstop while working on the same skill, you may start out well but will soon drop back to your old habit as your body tires and goes into survival mode. Instead of staying on the new pathway your brain will default to the old shortcut that requires less physical and mental energy.

Yes, it can be a bit boring and frustrating to keep things short and repetitive when you are enthused about becoming a better swimmer and just want to make progress, but, like any swim teacher or coach will tell you, it's the only way forward. Putting hours of work in using incorrect technique is a waste of your time and will ultimately leave you frustrated. Bunker down for the early sessions and get your core skills right and the later sessions will really see you hit your stride.

It is also important to keep working on the previous skill as you take on each new one. There's no point in getting skill number one right but letting it fall by the wayside when you get to skill number two. It's a constant building process as you go forward, which is why it's best to take your time instead of trying to rush through.

I have included some links to YouTube videos for particular skills on The Swim Guide website. You can find them at:
https://theswimguide.weebly.com/links

SKILL ONE – RELAXED BUBBLES

Q. What is the # 1 Stumbling Block to Adults Swimming Efficiently?
A. They Can't Breathe Properly.

Many adults assume that blowing bubbles is just something fun that kids do when they're learning how to swim. After all it's one of the first things children are taught in the water, right? There is a reason that children are taught to blow bubbles right from the get go – it's because bubbles are the absolute foundation of swimming efficiently. Forget having a beautiful, graceful stroke or a power kick, if you don't blow bubbles, you will never be able to swim to your best ability.

Q. So WHY are bubbles so important?
A. Because it's how you exhale in the water!

Think about it – if you are going for a walk do you hold your breath for six steps then quickly exhale and gulp in some air at the same time? Do you do that when you run? I doubt it. If you did, you would soon collapse in exhaustion. So why would you do that when you swim?

If you have never learnt how to blow bubbles properly or you know that you don't blow bubbles when you swim, that is the very first thing you need to work on. To maintain a steady breathing pattern, you need to blow slow, relaxed bubbles. To go back to the walking analogy do you breathe out in short, sharp gasps when you walk? I'm presuming you don't. So, if you blow big bubbles in sharp bursts, that is exactly what you're doing in the water.

It is essential to get your bubble blowing right early in the process of becoming a better swimmer. While it might seem too small a thing to make any difference in your overall swimming ability, remember it is the foundation elements of anything that make a good, finished product.

Relaxed bubbles will take some practice. Start by just ducking under in shallow water. Open your mouth slightly and gently exhale in a steady stream. You can also exhale out of your nose if you wish. Nasal bubbles tend to be a personal choice, it's great if you can do them but don't get hung up on them if you prefer not to. Blow bubbles until you feel your breath starting to run out (but not until you're gasping for air). Pop your head above the water, take a quick breath in, then duck back under and do the same thing again. Repeat this exercise several times until you feel confident.

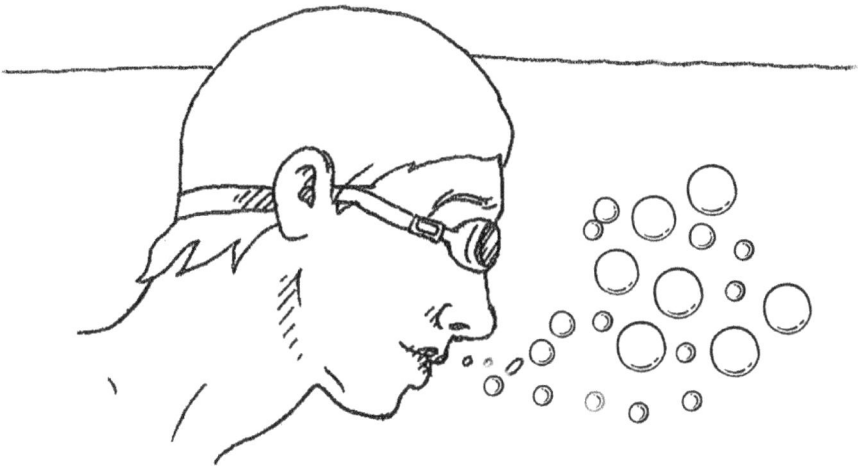

Next, swim a short distance underwater practising again some slow, relaxed bubbles. Make sure you're not creating a 'volcano' by releasing slowly to start with but erupting into a sharper expulsion as you get to the end of your exhale. This will take some getting used to and it is something you need to be conscious of until relaxed bubbles are second nature.

There is a video available for bubbles on the website links page.

SKILL TWO – CONQUER YOUR BREATHING

Now we have the bubbles under control, it's time to work on your breathing (that is, taking a breath as you swim). We will get to the rest of your freestyle technique a bit later – for now we just want to make sure you are inhaling and exhaling at maximum efficiency. It's a good idea to start in a smaller pool, if you can. A 50-metre pool can look very daunting when you are just starting out and it is easy to become discouraged if you can't make even one lap. If it has to be a 50-metre pool, work on a short distance first. Pick a spot you will swim to and stop there each time. It's also much easier if you start in the shallow end with your feet on the bottom.

As I mentioned earlier, I am assuming you have at least a basic freestyle stroke. It doesn't matter how messy or slow – just as long as you can move your arms and kick your legs. To swim efficiently you **have** to put your face in the water. There is absolutely no way around it. And, believe me, once you swim with your face in the water, you'll realise just how much easier it is. Besides, now that you have practised your slow, relaxed bubbles, having your face in the water should not be too difficult. (If you are scared to put your head under the water try my other book Learning To Swim When You're Scared: How to Overcome a Fear of Water. Its main focus is on learning to submerge.)

Your goal when swimming is to exhale all your air before you take your next breath. When I say all, I don't mean down to your absolute last gasp, but you should feel like you need to inhale again. Some coaches advocate a breathing method whereby you initially hold your breath, then slowly exhale. While I personally believe it easier to start your exhale as soon as your face goes in the water, I understand that for some people this breath hold method is easier. If you have either already learned to exhale this way or find my suggested method a challenge, by all means try this way instead. Whichever method you choose, however, the aim remains to exhale all your air by the time you turn to breathe.

A lot of people take a breath every second stroke. This is not a bad thing per se, but it is not the most efficient way to breathe when you swim. Why? Because turning to breathe while you swim creates drag in the water and slows down your stroke and forward momentum. Another theory is that breathing every second stroke does not let you exhale fully and you can get caught in a cycle of taking shallower breaths. For either reason, this means the less you have to breathe, the better. That is why I believe it is better to breathe every fourth stroke instead of every second. If you are used to breathing every two strokes, this will probably take some getting used to and you may initially struggle with it. But, trust me, if you persevere, you will probably be surprised at how much better you swim. This is not a hard and fast rule, though, so if you are really not comfortable breathing every fourth, then you should continue to breathe every second stroke. As you gain fitness, however, you may wish to try the four-stroke breathing again.

BILATERAL BREATHING

Generally most adult swimmers will breathe to their dominant side only (eg right handers turn to the right), but some are able to breathe on both sides (bi-lateral breathing). It is an advantage if you can breathe on both sides, but for a recreational swimmer it really doesn't matter if you can't. If you breathe bi-laterally you will breathe every third stroke by alternating sides each time you breathe. It can be a good balance between two and four stroke breathing, especially if you struggle to maintain breathing every four.

Bi-lateral breathing is a skill you can continue to work on as you practice swimming. Start out using flippers/fins or a pool buoy, just to give you some extra buoyancy. It does feel awkward breathing on the opposite side at first, but over time it will become more natural. You just have to practice a lot and retrain you brain. You will probably find that it never feels quite as easy on your weaker side, but an outside observer would not notice much difference. The advantage of learning bi-lateral breathing as an adult is that you can start with a clean slate for breathing on the opposite side. Unlike the side you have grown up with, which potentially has many bad habits deeply embedded. I will talk about the correct breathing technique in Skill Two.

Tip – To practice bi-lateral breathing, try breathing on the opposite side only for 50 or 100 metres at a time. During warm up or cool down is an ideal time to practice, as you are not focused on speed or other stroke elements. You can alternate with one lap your dominant side and one lap non-dominant. Once it feels like you're getting the hang of it, try alternate sides over shorter distances. Once you are comfortable breathing every four or three strokes it doesn't mean that is the only breathing pattern you have to follow. By all means mix it up a bit – especially if you are swimming fast or if you feel out of breath. It is easy to switch between different breathing patterns as you swim. You might still predominately swim breathing your preferred pattern but throw in some of the other patterns along the way.

BEYOND FOUR?

While breathing every four strokes is enough for most people, some swimmers like to push it out to five or six strokes. While this is a valuable skill to practise occasionally, it is not an efficient way to swim. You may start out able to breathe less when you're fresh, but you will fatigue quickly as your heart rate will climb. As mentioned earlier in the book, you want to take a breath just before you really need to. The only time you want to limit your breathing is during a sprint over a short distance. For example, to sprint twenty-five metres, you might be able to take ten or twelve strokes before breathing, but you wouldn't be able to maintain that over much more than that distance. In a fifty-metre sprint, limiting your breathing early on is achievable and will allow you to swim faster, but you will feel the effects of it by the time you reach the end. In a one hundred metre sprint, you may be able to get away with less breaths for a small part of that distance but not the whole way.

Begin with a short distance. Swim an easy/relaxed freestyle, making sure you start your relaxed bubbles as soon as your eyes go in the water. On the fourth stroke, roll your head to the side and take a quick inhalation of air. If you have been blowing your bubbles correctly you will not need to exhale at the same time. As soon as you've taken your breath roll your head back into the water and take another three strokes (while blowing relaxed bubbles) and breathe again on the fourth (or whatever you have chosen as your breathing pattern).

Make sure you do not lift your head out of the water (either forward or to the side). The breathing movement is a roll, not a lift. You should feel your ear on your shoulder (or close to it) as you breathe, and one eye of your goggles should remain in the water. When teaching kids, we refer to it as a 'sneaky' breath, meaning it should be as quick and unobtrusive as possible.

Continue this pattern until you get to your marker, then stop and have a rest. Practice this as much as you need to, until you are comfortable in this breathing pattern. You might want to do this for several sessions before you are competent. Although this might seem boring and repetitive, it will make things much easier as you progress through the technique skills. For some extra challenge, gradually increase your distance or start to build up some speed. You can also gradually decrease the rest time you have between each swim.

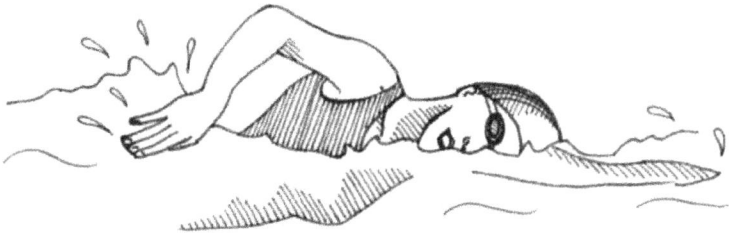

Roll your head and leave one goggle in the water.

SKILL THREE – EYES DOWN!

When you are at the stage where you can blow slow, relaxed bubbles and breathe every fourth stroke, you are ready to start tackling technique and distance. We will work on technique first. I am not promising to make you an Olympic champion with what I'm imparting here, but I will give you instructions to get the basics of your strokes correct.

The very first thing you should do when looking to improve your swimming technique is to get somebody to video you swimming. Don't freak out – it's not to be posted on YouTube so people can make fun of you – it's to give you an understanding of just what you're doing when you swim. Lots of swimmers (especially adults who've never had formal swimming instruction) think that their swimming technique is 'okay' or even 'good' when they are actually making fundamental errors. These errors can have a huge impact on your efficiency in the water.

 If you don't want to make a big deal of it, go to the pool when there are not many people there. You don't need any fancy video equipment – your regular digital camera or phone is fine. If you don't have somebody to take with you to video, there will almost certainly be a bystander or even a pool worker who can spare a minute or two to film you over about 25 metres. Film all the strokes you would like to get more proficient at. Make sure the video is taken close enough to be able to get a good, detailed look at the way you swim. If you do happen to have a GoPro or other waterproof camera, make use of it and get some underwater footage as well.

When you have your video, take some time to study it. If possible put it on a bigger screen than your phone – an iPad/tablet is good, as is a computer screen. You want to play it on a device that will allow you to pause, slow it down and generally manipulate it in a way that will allow you to become familiar with your swimming technique. It can be cringeworthy watching yourself on video, especially if your swimming style is not as good as you thought! However you have to move past this and study it objectively for maximum benefit. Don't worry, after several times watching it, you become less self-conscious.

The first thing you should look at is your head position. Is your head sitting high in the water or low? If it is high, it is almost certain that your eyes are looking forward. Next check your general body position. Is your body up on the surface of the water, including your legs? Or is the lower half of your body angled down with your legs much lower than your head? Don't worry if that is the case as I am about to tell you how to correct this fundamental (and common) error.

Body position is the foundation of all swimming strokes. The only way you can swim efficiently is to have a horizontal body position. Think about it in terms of four H's – head, hands, hips, heels. Each of these things need to be on the surface of the water if you wish to remain horizontal. To put it in simple physics terms, think about a boat on the water surface – will it move through the water efficiently if one end is higher than the other or if the middle sags down lower than the ends? Your body is the same. You just can't swim properly if your body is not horizontal in the water.

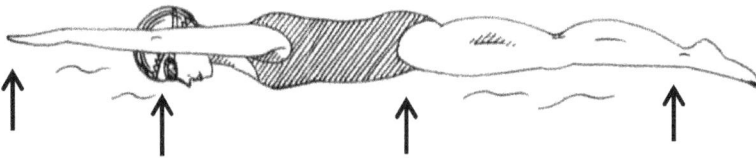

The four H's of body position.

The first common stumbling block to maintaining horizontal body position is looking ahead instead of looking to the bottom of the pool. Think about the way you swim – do your eyes look forward or down? Now check the video and see. You may be surprised at just how much you do look ahead. Even a small head tilt is enough to cause your hips (and legs) to drop. Furthermore only the front of your face should be in the water (from the ears down) – not your whole head.

Although looking ahead instead of down can initially be a hard habit to break, changing this will bring about a massive improvement in your swimming style.

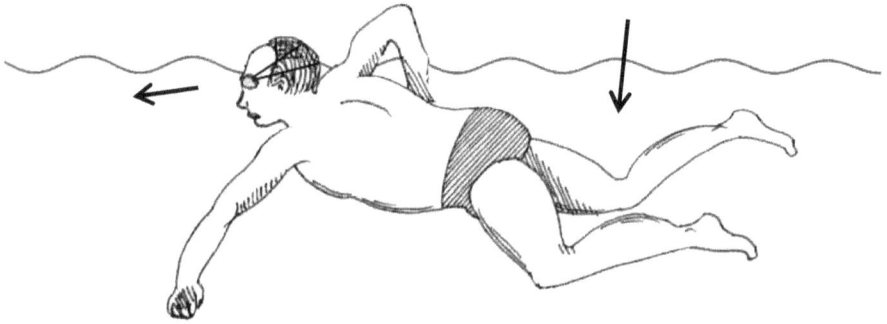

Tilting the head forward forces the legs down

Keep your video handy as you will be able to look at it each time we move onto a new element. If you are able to, update the video each time you improve a skill for a more accurate picture of what your stroke is doing as you move forward.

.

Swim 25 metres ensuring your eyes stay down the entire time. You need to be looking at the tiles on the bottom of the pool (or the black line most public pools have). Of course you can occasionally glance ahead (to see if you're getting close to the end for example) but do this quickly and without tilting your whole head forward. Think about having your spine in a neutral position rather than bending up or down.

Make sure you don't over-compensate and push your whole head under the surface of the water. You only want the front half of your head to submerge (from the ears down). You should be able to feel this fairly easily.

Swim with your eyes down enough times so that it becomes automatic. Say it as a mantra until you don't even need to think about it anymore. You need to have this skill down pat before you move onto the rest of your technique.

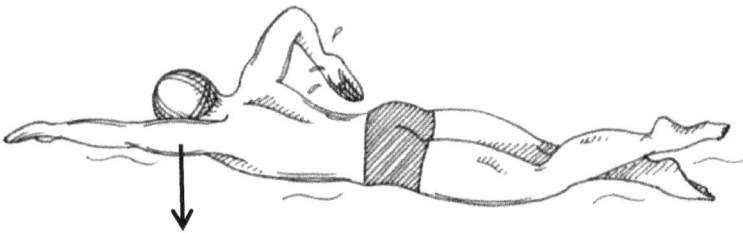

Always swim with your eyes to the bottom.

31

SKILL FOUR – WORK THAT KICK

Before we get into the specifics of kicking technique, I will mention a few points about adult swimmers and their kick. It is true that having a fast, efficient kick is an advantage in swimming and in an ideal world every swimmer would possess this skill. However, it is also true that most of the forward propulsion in freestyle comes from the stroke rather than the kick. (It's kind of like the back tyres on your car – they help but it's the front tyres that do most of the work). Some adults (especially women who are naturally more buoyant) can actually swim quite efficiently without kicking a lot (using what we call a two-beat kick, which is a slower, less regular kick). If your kick is not hindering your stroke (ie your knees are not bent or your legs are not too low in the water), you do not necessarily have to get too invested in trying to kick hard and fast. Your energies will probably be better put towards improving your stroke. The reality is that it is much easier to learn to kick efficiently as a child/adolescent, mainly due to body size and ankle flexibility. If you did swim squad as a kid then you will retain the skill, even if it takes a bit of time to get your muscle memory working. If not, it is unlikely you will be able to build up the same kind of strong, fast kick as a child/adolescent. As I just said, though, this does not have to be a major disadvantage for an adult swimmer.

In saying all that, however, your kick can definitely be improved and if you want to specifically work on your kick, then go right ahead. Use the same principals of repeatedly working the skill over a shorter distance, honing on technique rather than trying to grind out endless laps.

So, how are you supposed to kick?

To maintain a horizontal body position your kick must be at the surface of the water. There are two major reasons a swimmer's kick is not on the surface. We just spoke about your eyes needing to look at the bottom rather than in front. If you don't look at the bottom your head will be tilted forward, which will force your hips and legs down. Even the smallest amount of forward head tilt will make your hips and legs drop.

The second problem with kicking is bending your knees. The correct technique for a freestyle kick (also known as a flutter kick) is for your whole leg to move from the hip down. Your leg should be as straight as possible, with some flexibility in the knees (not rigid legs). Where the true flexibility should come is in your ankles. Your toes should be pointed when you kick (think of a ballerina standing on her toes) and to achieve this position your ankles need a fair degree of flexibility. Many adults struggle with ankle flexibility, especially if they have done a lot of running and cycling. Fortunately it is something that can be improved by doing specific exercises. One of the simplest is to simply practice sitting on your haunches for about ten minutes every day. For more specific exercise just google "ankle flexibility in swimming" or check with a physiotherapist.

As I mentioned above, women tend to have an advantage with kicking as they tend to be more buoyant in the water and as a result their body is already at the surface. Men, especially those who are more muscular, can struggle to keep their legs high. As long as your kick technique is correct, don't get too bogged down in trying to force your legs right up to the surface, focus instead of creating power in your arm stroke.

There is a video available for kicking on the website links page.

1. FIX BODY POSITION

If your problem with kicking is in your body position, there are two easy ways to practice getting it right. The first is called the streamline position. It is the way a swimmer starts their freestyle stroke either as a dive in or from pushing off the side. The streamline (sometimes called a torpedo or rocket in children's lessons) is the ideal body position in the water. It involves having your arms extended straight in front of you, with your arms pressing against your ears. Your hands should be flat with one pressed on top of the other. Your legs should be long and straight and your eyes should be looking to the bottom. If you struggle to get your arms into the streamline position, practice on dry land. Like yoga poses, if you gradually work towards it and repeat several times a day you will soon be able to do it.

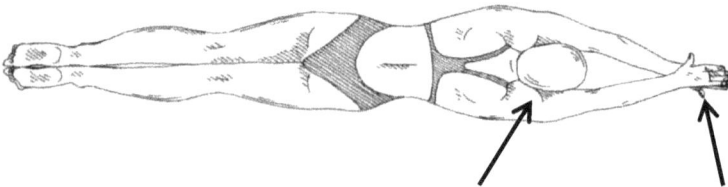

The correct streamline position (aerial view). Arms on ears and hands together.

Practice pushing off the side and kicking over a short distance in streamline position. You should be able to physically feel your feet splashing on the surface. Stop when you need to take a breath, then kick again. This is a skill best practised in shallow water as you need to be able to push off from a standing position.

The second method is to use a kickboard. Take a kickboard and grasp it at the flat, bottom end (thumb underneath and fingers on top). Now push off and kick with your eyes facing the bottom. Ensure your arms are straight. Push your bottom up, rather than letting it sag down. Try to make your toes touch lightly by adopting a slightly pigeon toed foot position. You should feel your feet splashing on the surface.

Kicking on a kickboard is difficult to begin with, so focus on a shorter distance (15 to 25 metres). When you feel you are proficient have yourself videoed again to make sure you are kicking on the surface with straight legs and loose ankles.

Push bottom up   **Keep arms straight**

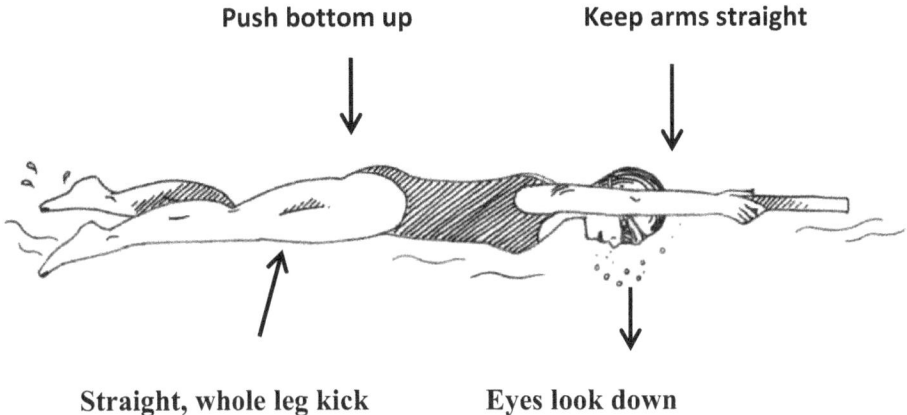

Straight, whole leg kick   **Eyes look down**

2. UNBEND THOSE KNEES!

Correcting a bent knee kicking technique is more of a challenge, but not impossible There are a couple of methods you can try. The first is to use fins/flippers. As I mentioned before the use of flippers is a double-edged sword. On the plus side you will notice a huge, immediate improvement to your kick. Why? Because they force your feet to the surface, which will keep your legs relatively straight. On the minus side, flippers can become addictive. You can get so used to the aided flotation and extra speed that going back to swimming without them can make your legs feel like lead. Refer to the section earlier in the book about flippers for more information on which kind to choose and how best to use them. For kicking practice I would recommend using shorter flippers as they provide resistance on both the up and down kick and also feel like a more natural kicking style.

If you decide to use flippers, use them sparingly. Kick on the kickboard as outlined above until you really get the feel of a straight legged kick from the hip down. This may take several sessions. You can also practice swimming freestyle with the flippers on. After practising with the flippers, video yourself again and make sure you are kicking with a straight leg. If you have reverted to a bent knee, start the process again. As tedious as this may seem, you have to get your kick right before you have a hope of improving your overall technique, as well as increasing the distance you can swim.

If you don't have any flippers available to you or would prefer not to use them, there are a couple of other things you can do. The first is to sit on the edge of the pool and practice a kicking motion. Being able to see your legs will ensure you are keeping them straight. Point your toes like a ballerina to create a long, streamlined leg position.

Another way to work on your kick is to practice a sideways, scissoring motion. Take a kickboard and extend your arm straight over it, grasping the kickboard at the round (top) end with your fingers and thumb wrapping over the edge. Lean your ear on your shoulder and begin to move through the water with your body in a side on position (belly button facing the wall). Kick your legs in a scissor like motion, back and forth. The advantage of being on your side is that you can see your legs and have an awareness of what they are doing. Practice until you are proficient and then try regular kick again.

A third way to work on your kick is to start on your back. Lying on your back in the water, grasp a kickboard onto your chest by wrapping your arms around it in a hugging fashion. Point your toes like a ballerina and work on a slow, whole-leg kick, making sure your feet are creating a small splash on the surface of the water. If you cannot feel the splash, your feet are not high enough. When you feel that you have become proficient, try kicking on the kickboard again in the normal fashion. Get yourself filmed and ensure your legs are not bending and are at the surface of the water.

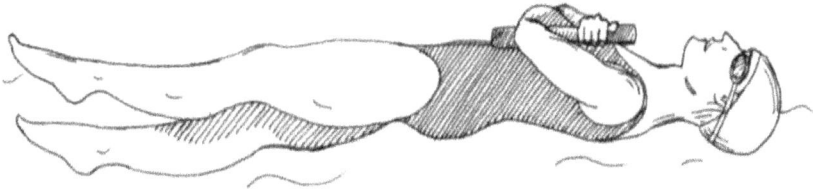

Kicking on the back can be helpful

One final suggestion if you are really struggling is to fashion a kind of knee brace to keep your legs relatively straight as you kick. Remember we don't want them rigid, so there needs to be some movement in the knee. A neoprene knee brace, for example, can be helpful with this. It is all about rewiring your brain from one old habit to a new one. If you do use this suggestion, use the brace for several weeks as you swim, just to really enforce new muscle memory.

.

PUTTING IT ALL TOGETHER

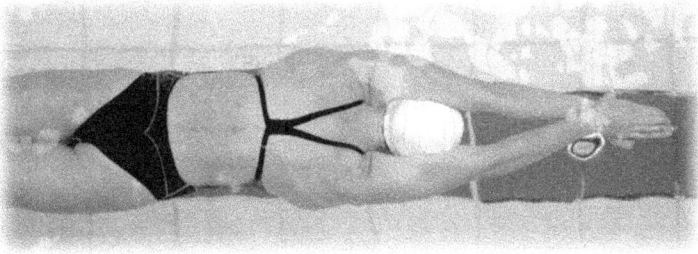

- ✪ Phases of freestyle
- ✪ Rotation
- ✪ Use Of Pull Buoy

SKILL FIVE – THE WHOLE STROKE

Once you have your bubbles, breathing, kick and body position sorted out you are ready to progress onto the other elements of freestyle technique. Congratulations on making it this far! It takes patience and persistence to get those core elements right, but the good news is that the next stage should be easier. I do not want to get too technical here, as it is not my aim to confuse or bamboozle you with too much information. However, understanding the mechanics of the freestyle stroke will help you comprehend what you are trying to achieve.

In simplest terms to swim efficient freestyle you need to take long strokes and also rotate your body as you stroke, rather than keeping your body flat and just moving your arms and legs. Your arms should move continuously and opposite (one arm in and one arm out at the same time).

Begin freestyle in a streamline position. When you push off from the wall, your arms should be extended straight and locked over your ears. Your hands should be placed flat on top of one another. This is the optimum body position to get the best possible start for your stroke. Watch how any competitive swimmer starts their race – that is the body position you are aiming for. Kick a few times in this position to give yourself some forward momentum before you start stroking.

After pushing off your first arm will move underneath your body. Rather than pushing your arm straight through the water windmill style, you should bend your elbow as you point your fingers down towards the bottom. Sweep your hand and forearm slightly inwards towards your torso. Once past the mid-point of your torso push your hand back out and down the length of your body until the arm is straight again. Brush your hand past your leg (just below the hip) as it prepares to exit the water.

Bend your elbow after your arm exits the water. Then lift and move the arm forward and extend it in line with your shoulder and have it enter the water at about two thirds extension (fingertips enter first). Once your hand is in the water you then extend your arm fully. From there you move back to the start, with the elbow bending and your arm moving back under your body.

The other element of freestyle is a continual rotation of your body from the shoulders down. The only thing that stays still is your head (except when breathing). When you breathe you use this rotation to roll your head to the side and inhale. Rotation is not as difficult as it sounds – if you lead with your shoulder, the rest of you will follow. The simplest way to think of it is 'one shoulder up, one shoulder down.' The shoulder that is up is the arm that is out of the water and the shoulder that is down is the arm underneath.

When your arm is fully extended under the water your body is at maximum rotation. To achieve maximum rotation the shoulder of your leading arm should be well below the water level and the shoulder of the opposite arm should be completely out of the water.

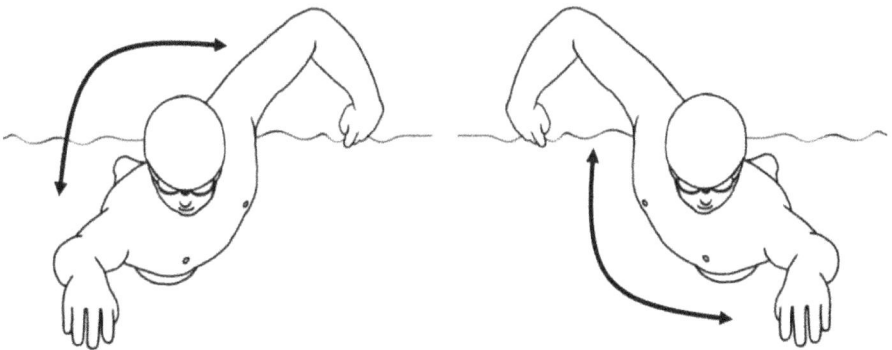

Continual body rotation is an important element of freestyle.

Also remember during freestyle you need to maintain the whole leg flutter kick, have your eyes facing the bottom (except when breathing) and be exhaling your breath with slow, relaxed bubbles.

GETTING A BIT MORE TECHNICAL

The following pages are for those who wish to get a bit more technical with their understanding of the freestyle stroke. If you find it too confusing to begin with don't worry too much about it now and work with the more basic information in the previous section.

There are considered to be four phases of the freestyle stroke:

1. The Catch – when your hand first enters the water.
2. The Pull – the action of your arm as it moves under the water beneath your body.
3. The Exit – when your arm brushes past your leg and lifts out of the water.
4. The Recovery – when your arm is in the air moving back towards entering the water again.

Going back to the information on the previous pages you can relate these phases to what I previously explained.

I will now use a series of pictures to illustrate each phase of the stroke. Even though the catch is technically the first phase, I will start here with the pull as if you are starting in streamline position the pull is the first part you will do.

The Pull

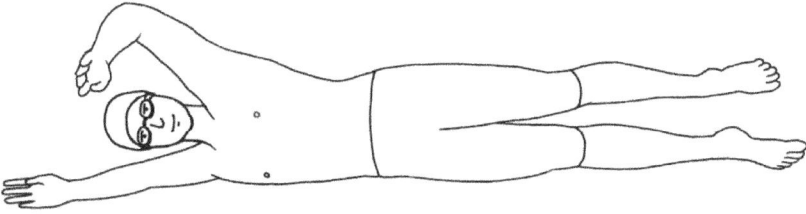

Bend your elbow and point your fingers down as the arm moves underneath your body. Ensure the elbow is always higher than the wrist. Sweep the forearm slightly inwards and then upwards towards the torso.

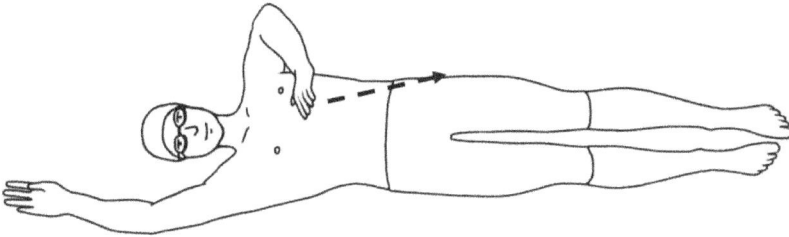

Push your hand back, out and up until it straightens and your thumb brushes past your thigh. Throughout the pull phase you should concentrate on pushing the water back with your hand. The palm should face backwards right from the time it starts moving down from the surface of the water.

The Exit

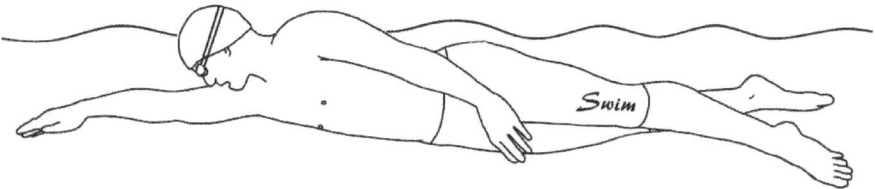

Extend your arm straight and brush your thumb past your leg just below the hip before exiting. Try to avoid flicking your hand as it exits.

The Recovery

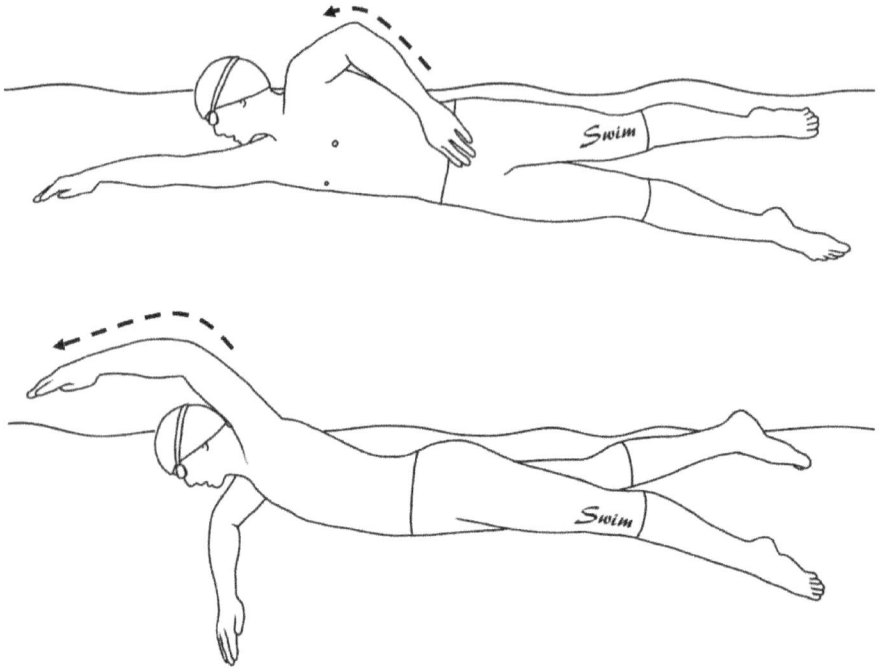

Bend your elbow and lift your arm out of the water before extending it forwards in line with your shoulder. Make sure that your body is rotating as the arm is lifting.

A note about bent elbow recovery:

Even though bending the elbow is considered to be the technically correct way to complete the freestyle stroke (and is generally the way it is taught), this is not an absolute rule. Some elite swimmers swim with a straight arm recovery and a more "swinging" stroke style. (Olympian Michael Klim is an example). So if you are of those people who has a straight arm recovery and it feels a more natural way for you to swim, then go with it. The main thing you need to be aware of is to not use a straight arm in the underwater pull phase as this creates much more resistance and will slow your stroke down.

The Catch

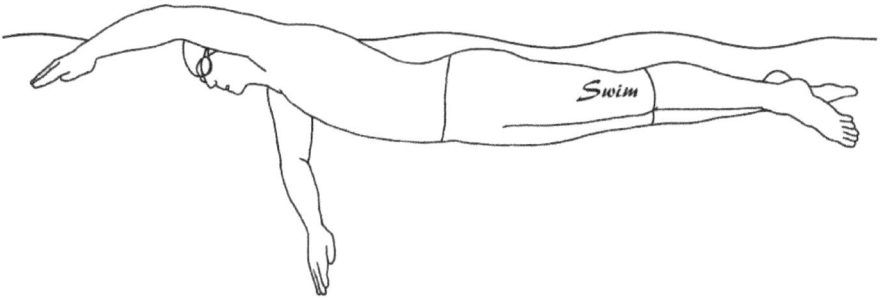

Your hand should enter the water with the arm at two thirds extension and in line with your shoulder. Your fingertips should enter the water first (not the thumb). Your hand should enter the water softly, rather than with a heavy splashing motion.

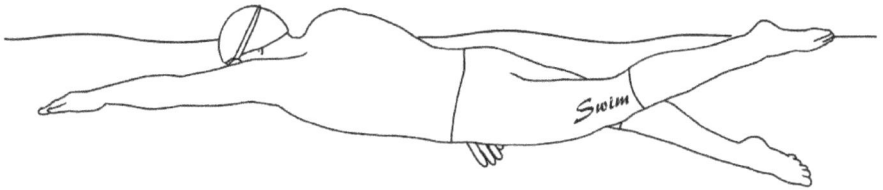

Once in the water your arm should stretch out to full extension and your body should be at maximum rotation.

COMMON PITFALLS IN THE FREESTYLE STROKE

While every swimmer is different and there are potentially hundreds of different errors that can occur during freestyle, generally there are a few common ones that many swimmers do. None of these are too complex, they will just require awareness on your part. If you are making several errors, just work on one at a time rather than trying to correct everything at once. Remember when you first try to change something in your stroke it will feel wrong to begin with. You are attempting to unpick long held habits and it does take concentration and effort to recalibrate that part of your brain.

THE HAND ENTERING TOWARDS THE MIDLINE OF THE BODY

Sometimes it can be over the midline, creating an almost zigzag stroke. Study your video to check your hand placement. If you do cross over, practice over a short distance and really exaggerate placing your hand wide. As the hand being in the middle feels normal to you, it is necessary to go wider than you think you need to in order to correct. If you have someone check your hand placement or get it videoed, you will find that what feels wide is, in fact, where it should be (in line with your shoulder). This is an occasion where it is okay to look ahead and see where your fingers are entering the water. Check your rotation too as under rotating can cause the hand to cross over. Also check that your fingers are entering first and not your thumb.

UNDER ROTATING

There are a few reasons why it is much more efficient to rotate your body when you swim freestyle. The first of these is the length of your stroke. Rotating with your leading shoulder under the water allows that arm to reach further forward for each stroke. Ultimately this means you will take less strokes over any distance. Similar to running, it uses much less energy to perform 40 long strokes/strides over say 50 metres than

90 short ones. The short ones might make you look like you're moving faster but will wear you out much quicker.

The second reason is that it allows you to use your larger core muscles to create forward movement in the water, rather than having to rely only on your shoulder muscles (which are smaller and weaker).

The third reason is injury. Lying flat in the water and relying only on the shoulder muscles for forward momentum places a lot of strain on these muscles as it is a very awkward movement. Even if you stretch before swimming and warm up properly in the water, performing this action over and over will almost certainly eventually lead to straining and inflammation of the shoulder muscles at some point. Swimmer's Shoulder is a well-known injury caused by incorrect freestyle technique and can take a long time to heal.

You guessed it, slowing your stroke down and performing it over a shorter distance will allow you to focus on the position of your body as your swim. Think about one shoulder in and one out of the water as you take each stroke. Once you are aware of the action it will start to feel more natural and over time will become second nature as you swim. Don't worry too much about over rotating – it is much more common in children rather than adults. But if you feel like you are rolling almost to your back when you breathe or that your stroke stops and starts a bit then you may be rotating too far. In that case dial it back just a little and you should find the correct balance.

SHORT STROKES

A short stroke occurs when the hand enters the water before the arm reaches two thirds extension. Given that the elbow will be bent at that point it is very difficult to then extend the arm fully. As discussed above, taking lots of short strokes is a very inefficient way to swim and results in a choppy stroke that will eventually leave you exhausted. A short stroke is something you should fix before moving onto distance swimming. Practice swimming freestyle using a kickboard to get the feel of extending your arm further. Hold the kickboard with one arm while the other strokes, switching arms as you go. You can also do a drill using a completely straight arm in the recovery phase to get out of the habit of bending the elbow too much. Practice this over 25 metres (six times) and then revert to bent arm again.

The finish of the stroke can also be short. When the arm exits the water, it should be close to full extension, meaning your thumb should brush your thigh on the way past. Many adult swimmers exit their hand closer to the waist, shortening the stroke length substantially. The simplest way to work on this flaw is to consciously feel for your thumb to touch your thigh as it exits the water. If you can't feel your thumb on your leg you have exited too early.

When you feel like you have corrected a short stroke, have yourself filmed again to check that you have increased your stroke length. You can also count how many strokes you are taking per lap, as you increase your stroke length, the number of strokes you take over fifty metres should decrease.

Dropping The Opposite Arm While Breathing

As mentioned in the breathing section, when you roll to breathe, your ear should touch your shoulder (or close to it). For many adult swimmers, however, their leading arm drops before they roll to breathe, leaving nothing for the head to balance on when it rolls. The flow on effect of this is the head lifting and the legs dropping. Use fins or a pull buoy to keep your legs high and focus solely on your stroke. Make sure the opposite arm remains high until you have taken a breath. A good drill to work on this is to kick (with fins) with one arm extended and the other down by your side. Breathe as required (rolling the head towards the arm that is by the side), focusing on the ear touching the shoulder each time.

Note: In the past swimmers were sometimes taught to trace an 'S' pattern during the underwater phase with the thumb entering the water first. The general consensus these days is that the S pattern is not the most efficient way to swim freestyle and can, in fact, lead to shoulder injury (as the thumb first action leads to internal rotation of the shoulder joint). Ultimately though if you have learned that way and you feel that it works for you stick with it at least initially. Perhaps as your fitness and overall stroke improves you may want to consider altering your underwater technique.

HELPFUL APP

To get an extremely comprehensive view of the correct way the freestyle stroke should be performed there is a wonderful app available at both the iTunes and Android app stores. It is called **Mr Smooth** and although it is more expensive than the average app, it is certainly worth the still modest price tag. Mr Smooth allows you to study the freestyle stroke from every imaginable angle to get the whole picture and can be slowed right down to a snail's pace so you can study each phase in detail. I use Mr Smooth myself with my students to show them what they are aiming for in their stroke. It is best viewed on an iPad or tablet to get a bigger picture, but also works well on the average smart phone. If you do not have a tablet or smart phone you can see Mr Smooth on the Swim Smooth website. (www.swimsmooth.com).

PRACTICE THIS...

There is a lot to remember when working the whole freestyle stroke, which is why I emphasised the need to get the breathing, body position and kick correct first. You can start with flippers, if you like, to ensure you have the correct body position while consolidating your stroke, then transition to no flippers.

Yep, once again, swim the whole stroke over a short distance (25 metres), then have a short rest (around 20 or 30 sec). Repeat it as many times as you need to really get the stroke right. You do not need to swim fast, nor do you need to go a long distance yet. Work on each element in order, focusing on getting one right before moving onto the next.

Ask yourself if you are rotating your body and brushing your hand back past your leg each time you take a stroke. Is your elbow bending as it moves (pulls) underneath your body? Is your hand entering the water in line with your shoulder and at two thirds extension (not before)? Are your eyes looking to the bottom? Is your head nice and low as you roll to breathe?

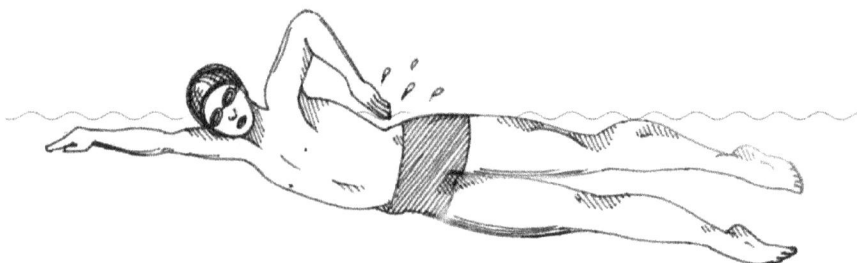

The whole freestyle stroke involves a lot of different elements

After working on your stroke for a while, have yourself filmed again and study your technique. Are you hitting all the targets? If you aren't, work on those elements that you haven't quite mastered. If possible slow your video down so you can get a clear picture of all the different elements of your stroke.

USE OF PULL BUOY

A pull buoy is a small, figure eight shaped piece of foam designed to sit between your thighs (as high as is comfortable). Its purpose is to force your legs to the surface of the water, thus providing a perfect horizontal body position. Like flippers, pull buoys can be addictive if used too often, so use them sparingly.

Pull buoys come in a range of shapes and sizes. Unless you are a very slight build you should aim to get a pull buoy that is large enough to provide adequate flotation. This is particularly important for men. Some of the smaller, slimline types are not sufficient to keep a male of average build's legs afloat.

When you use a pull buoy make sure you don't kick. If you find it difficult to not kick, use an ankle band to keep your ankles together. An ankle band is a large rubber band you place around your ankles to keep them together. Some pools have them to borrow but you can also get them in sports stores or on-line. Alternatively you can make your own from the inner tube of a tyre. They are long lasting and very durable. If making your own band, ensure that you can fit both ankles inside comfortably with a little wriggle room. Ankle bands are not intended to be too firm.

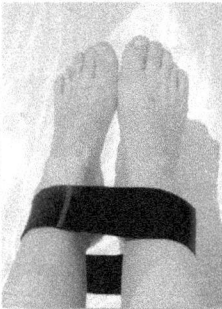

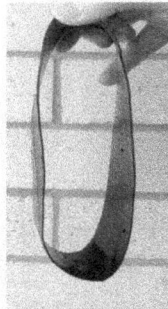

Ankle bands can be made from tyre inner tube.

The main aim when using a pull buoy is to work on your stroke technique. Really concentrate on long strokes, proper breathing technique and a nice body rotation.

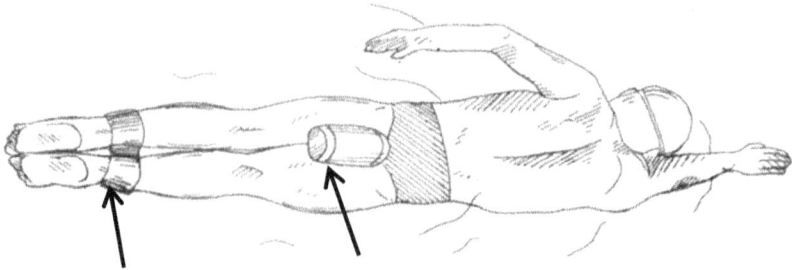

Ankle band   Pull Buoy

USE OF ANKLE BAND ONLY

Another way to really test if your body position is correct is to swim using an ankle band (as described above) without a pull buoy. Theoretically if your body position is correct you should be able to swim reasonably comfortably with your feet on or near the surface of the water. Naturally it will take more energy than swimming with kicking, but it is a good challenge to try occasionally. Don't panic if your feet sink – lots of swimmers (even some who are very proficient) struggle with this drill. But it is a good thing to practice regularly and chart your progress to see if you improve.

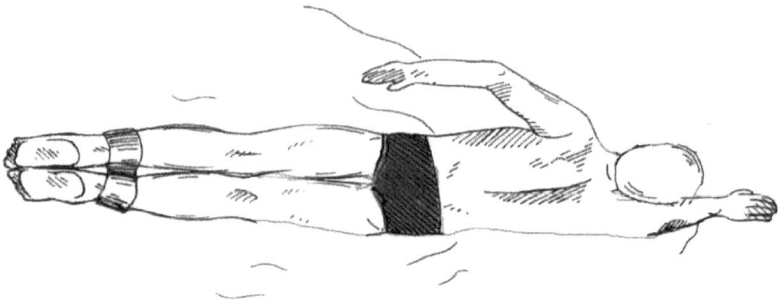

GOING THE DISTANCE

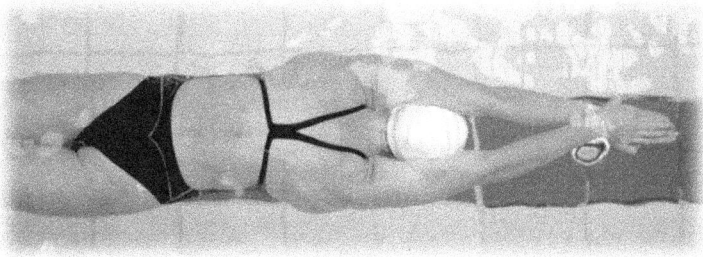

- ✪ Drills
- ✪ Staying Effecient
- ✪ Doing Laps

SKILL SIX – DOING LAPS

Once you are happy with how you are completing the freestyle stroke, you can finally tackle some distance work. No doubt you have already improved the distance you are able to swim, not to mention the efficiency of your stroke. But remember, like any physical endeavour, it will take time to build up your fitness. Don't become discouraged if you are only able to cover a short distance to begin with. The key to swimming further is to gradually build your distance over time.

Start in a 25 metre pool if possible. Set a goal of how many laps you would like to swim for your first session. Ten laps is probably a good starting point. When you are swimming laps always aim to complete a whole lap, no matter how tired or out of breath you may become. Stopping in the middle of a lap is a bad habit to get into. When teaching children, I tell them there are sharks or crocodiles at the bottom that will snap their feet if they stop. You could use the same analogy.

Have a set rest period between each lap. Thirty seconds is a good starting point (perhaps extending to 45 seconds towards the end of your session). Use either your own watch or the pace clock at the pool (all public pools will have one). Don't wait until you are completely rested before starting your next lap, as you will not improve your fitness this way. Maintain the set rest period unless you are absolutely exhausted or have a cramp or a stitch. Even if you have to swim at a snail's pace, keep going to the end of each lap. You do need to push yourself to build endurance. As your fitness improves you can cut down the rest period between each lap.

The more often you swim in the early stages, the quicker your improvement will be. Ideally if you could swim five to seven days for the first few weeks, your improvement will be fast and noticeable. As you become more proficient, you can drop back to three or four sessions (and eventually less) to maintain a reasonable level of fitness.

Each day you swim, you should be building on both your distance and your speed. Try to increase the distance you swim in each block (for example 50 metres without stopping, then 100 metres, then 150 metres and so on) each day. But also increase the overall distance you do. You might start out at 500 metres, then move to 750 metres, then 1 kilometre and so on. Each session should include a warm up, a main set and a warm down. The warm up/warm down is designed to wake your muscles up and cool them down and the main set is where the harder work is done.

You don't have to make massive improvements in your speed, but you should start to swim a little faster as your fitness improves. Keep an eye on your watch or the pace clock and challenge yourself to swim slightly faster each time. To further increase your speed, you should also include some sprints in your workout. You can start with 25 metres and build to 50. For that distance you need to go as fast as you can possibly go over that distance. You only need to do two or three sprints each session and you can allow yourself a longer rest period between them (up to one minute). If you practice a sprint each session, you will notice a fairly rapid improvement to begin with. Remember when you are trying to swim fast, you still want to maintain those core elements you have worked on earlier – you are just trying to speed everything up. This means kicking harder and faster and moving your arms faster.

It can be a bit boring just swimming laps by yourself. It can also be uninspiring just swimming lap after lap of freestyle. So you will either need to mix your workouts up a bit to keep yourself motivated or maybe convince some friends to come along with you. You could also join an organised squad (or at least swim at the same time as an organised squad. Check out what they do in their session to gain some ideas). I have included some suggested sessions at the end of this book. You will get the idea of how to put together a training session. A mix of sprints and distance is ideal. It is rare that you would get in the pool and just swim a straight 2km, instead you might do some one hundreds, then some fifties or some two hundreds and so on. You do not need to swim continuously at the same pace to gain fitness, the key is to have regular rest breaks but make them a set time (for example 10/15/20 seconds). Again, though, if you check out the suggested sets at the end of the book you will see what I mean. It is a good idea to either print out or write your set and take it with you. Put it in a plastic sleeve to keep dry and sit it on the end of the pool with your gear. That way you can keep track of what you are doing.

As well as taking time to gain fitness, it can also take time to get into a rhythm when you swim. I know myself that the first lap when I start a session feels great, but then I feel a bit sluggish over the next few until I get my breathing really sorted out. Once you find that rhythm though, you will feel like you can go on indefinitely. That is why having a warm up at the start of your session is necessary, it lets your body get into the swing of swimming.

Most of your swimming will be done at a moderate pace. This means you should be pushing yourself a bit. So you won't be swimming slowly and your heart rate will be higher than normal but you are not going flat out. You should be able to speak normally at the end of a lap without puffing. Remember too that you need to set your own goals based on your physical limitations and what you are doing swimming for. In all honesty if you come to the pool and do twenty laps of very slow breaststroke it will probably not increase your fitness much. Sure, any activity is good for you, but you do need to push yourself at least a little and get your heart rate up at least part of the time to gain real benefit.

Once you have built up some fitness, make sure you keep swimming regularly. Anything less than two sessions per week and you will notice some regression in your speed and the distance you are able to swim.

Staying Efficient

When you swim you should aim to be as efficient as you can. This means you should complete each lap using as few strokes as possible. The more strokes you take the more energy you burn and the more fatigued you will become, which will then make you take more strokes and get even tireder!

A very simple way to test your efficiency is to count your strokes. Over 50 metres the average adult recreational swimmer will probably take anywhere from 50 to 70 strokes – but don't get too hung up on the number – what you are aiming for is consistency. So if your number is 58 – then each time you swim a lap either at the beginning or end of your training session your stroke count should still be around that number. Obviously a difference of three or four strokes is not a big deal, but anything more than that would suggest that you need to work on stroke efficiency. You don't need to count strokes every lap, but aim to do so four or five times during a training session. Keep a record in your training diary.

Two key ways to improve your stroke count are to rotate properly and finish your stroke down past your hip. Adding just a small distance per stroke using these methods adds up over each lap. A caveat to improving your stroke count is to make sure you don't artificially slow your stroke down by pausing before your hand exits or over-gliding as your hand enters the water. Doing either of these things will create a whole new set of problems and neither are sustainable over distance.

Lane Etiquette

When swimming in a public pool it is more than likely that you will have to share a lane with other swimmers. Generally pools will have lanes designated for laps and will also categorise them as slow, medium and fast. When sharing a lane, it is important to follow lane etiquette by swimming on either the left or right side of the lane (this varies by country). This allows swimmers to keep moving without causing collisions. Use the black line on the bottom as the lane mid-point. If you cross it you are too far over.

If somebody wants to pass you, allow them to. Passing simply involves them swimming out around you and then back in front. Similarly if you need to pass somebody do the same – allow a wide enough margin that you will not bang into them, but also check in front of you to make sure you won't collide with a swimmer coming the other way. The other option is to wait until you get to the end and simply move in front of the other swimmer. It is great if you get a lane to yourself but it probably won't happen very often in a public pool. Be prepared to share.

PACE CLOCK

The pace clock is a large clock (normally analogue but sometimes digital) with a continuous second hand. It allows you to time yourself by checking your start and finish times on the clock. One end of the second hand will be red and the other black (which allows you to keep track of if you start on the black 60 second or red). Many pools will have one at both ends, smaller pools may only have one, but they are always located in a highly visible spot either at the deep or shallow end.

FREESTYLE DRILLS

There are many different drills you can practice to work on various elements of your freestyle stroke. While these drills can seem quite difficult and make your feel unco-ordinated, they are very helpful in isolating various parts of the freestyle stroke and helping you to improve your whole stroke. Remember too that a drill will often exaggerate a certain aspect of your stroke just while doing the drill. This can help break a bad habit and bring you back to the middle of the pendulum.

The point of drills is to slow things down, so don't feel like you have to swim fast. In fact, you should make an effort to swim slower than normal. It is also a very good idea to wear flippers, as the extra buoyancy will allow you to focus all your attention on the skill in question, rather than on trying to stay afloat. Single arm freestyle, for example, is almost impossible to complete correctly without fins.

To get the most out of drills, do them for a short time only during a swimming session and then link it back to your freestyle stroke. There is no point doing laps and laps of drills if you revert back to doing the exact same thing you were doing before. A good rule of thumb is to do a drill for one lap, then freestyle for a lap, really thinking about what you just practised, be it breathing, rotation or stroke.

To practice the breathing action, try the following drills. Using flippers/fins is recommended. See the later section on flippers/fins for more information about choosing the correct pair.

* Hold a kickboard at the lower end with both hands and kick and blow bubbles. When you need to take a breath, roll your head to the side and use your breathing arm only to complete one arm stroke. If you breathe on one side only, the only arm that moves will be your breathing arm. If you breathe both sides, alternate your arms for each breath. **Drill #1**

- Hold a kickboard with your left hand only on the lower edge. Place your right arm down by your side. Kick and blow bubbles. When you need to take a breath roll your head and rotate your body until your right shoulder lifts out of the water. Roll back when you have taken your breath. Alternate between both arms. You can also do this drill without the kickboard, with just one arm extended. **Drill #2**

- Expand your breathing pattern – start at four strokes per breath, then move to six and then eight (or three, five and seven). You can't sustain this for a long period, but over three or four laps it is a good way to train yourself to breathe as efficiently as possible. **Drill #3**

To Work on your arm stroke:

- Catch Up Freestyle – In this form of freestyle you wait for each arm to 'catch up' before the next arm begins its stroke (rather than continuous arms). Begin with both arms in front of you, shoulder width apart – then do your first stroke and when that arm returns to the start position, do your next stroke with the other arm. Each time you stroke ensure you are extending your arm fully when it enters the water and pushing back past your leg when it exits again.

- Single Arm Freestyle – swim freestyle using one arm only. The other arm must stay down by your side. Aim to breathe every third stroke and complete a long, efficient stroke with body rotation each time. This is quite a difficult (but effective) drill – to make it easier use fins.

- Finger Trail – swim freestyle but instead of doing a normal recovery motion, drag your thumb along your side, right up to your armpit, before completing the stroke as normal. This allows you to work on a high elbow recovery.

OTHER STROKES AND FURTHER INFORMATION

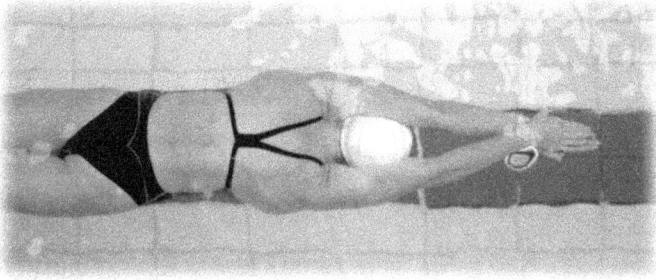

- ✪ Backstroke
- ✪ Breaststroke
- ✪ Diving and Tumble Turns
- ✪ Ocean and Open Water

BACKSTROKE

Swimming efficient backstroke also requires a horizontal body position. Just like freestyle, as soon as your head lifts or tilts even slightly, your hips and legs will drop down.

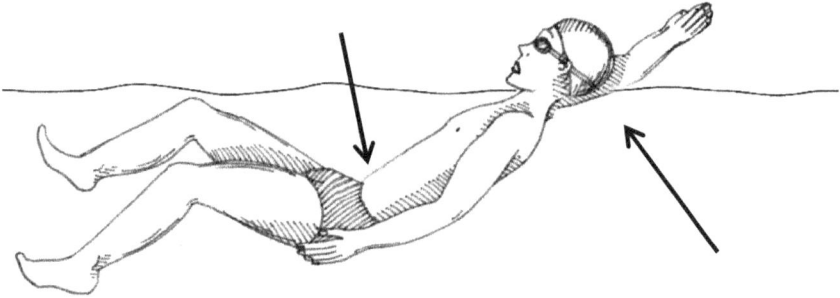

When your head lifts your hips and legs drop.

THE KICK

First practice kicking on your back. Your head needs to be flat in the water, so you are looking at the roof or the sky. Either have your hands above your head in a streamlined position or down by your side. Just like freestyle, your kick needs to start from the hip and your legs need to be straight (with some slight knee flexibility). Your toes should be pointed and you should feel them splash at the surface.

 If you find that your legs are sinking, you can practice with a kickboard first. Hold the board on your chest and wrap your arms around it. Kick at least 25 metres, concentrating on feeling your feet splash at the surface. Practice this until you are proficient, then try without the board again. Have somebody film you so you can check your body position is correct.

If you get water over your face and up your nose you are tilting your head back too far. The water should lap just around your ears. Lift your head slightly and try again. Keep working on it until you can keep your face relatively dry.

THE STROKE

When you are happy with your kick you can introduce the arms. Your arm will start from down by your side – raise it up straight, lifting your shoulder as you go. Your arm should brush straight past your ear, then go down behind your head and enter the water with your little finger first. There are two ways you can finish the stroke. The old-fashioned way is to simply complete a full circle with your arm (windmill fashion) under the water until it reaches your leg and continues onto the next stroke. The newer way is to bend your elbow once your arm enters the water and then push it back to your side. Experiment and decide which way works best for you. Either way your fingers should be straight and together.

Your arm must always touch your ear to do backstroke correctly. If you can't feel it brush past on every stroke you need to adjust your arm movement.

Your arms need to move in a continuous and opposite motion (ie one arm going in and one coming out at the same time). Your kick should be continuous throughout the stroke – if not your feet will start sinking and your arms will have to work much, much harder to propel you through the water.

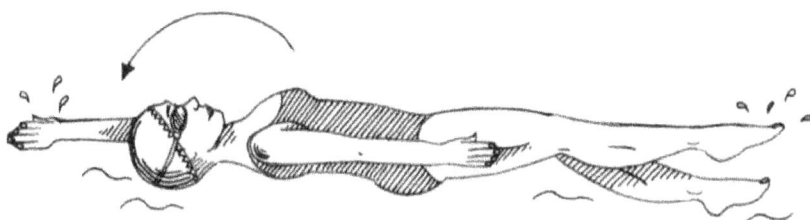

Keep your head flat and your legs on the surface.

A common issue with backstroke is moving in a zig-zag fashion across your pool lane rather than in a straight line. (You should see kids practising – avoiding collisions can be a full-time job!). To keep straight remember that the head steers the body. If your head leans to the right, the rest of you will follow. If you are in an indoor pool, see if there is a line on the roof you can follow. Otherwise use your lane ropes or the pool edge as a guide. You should be within touching distance at all times, if you notice the gap is widening, it means you are drifting. Simply correct your position and keep moving.

Backstroke is a good way to keep moving when you are tired or out of breath. You will keep momentum but get a chance to recover.

BREASTSTROKE

Breaststroke is often seen as the fall-back stroke for adults. When it becomes too difficult to continue swimming freestyle, most people will revert to breaststroke. Additionally, breaststroke is also the stroke that the general public believe they can swim reasonably well. While they may be able to propel themselves through the water in a style resembling breaststroke, very few adults can do the stroke in a technically correct fashion. I know myself, that until I was shown a video of my breaststroke kick at age twenty-one, I sincerely believed I was doing it properly. I wasn't! Seeing that video allowed me to fix it.

Just like freestyle you have to put your head under the water to do breaststroke properly. However as you breathe every stroke you will find that you don't get out of breath like you can in freestyle. You still need to blow bubbles and your eyes need to look at the bottom.

THE KICK

We'll start with the kick. Have yourself filmed doing breaststroke kick and watch the footage. Do both your feet turn out as they kick around? Don't worry if they don't – you are definitely not alone. The most common error in the breaststroke kick is having only one foot turned out, while the other flings itself over in the same direction as the first foot, rather than the opposite (a 'screw' kick). The main issue with the screw kick is that it provides no forward propulsion, which, naturally enough, will slow you down considerably. It can take some effort and concentration to correct a dodgy breaststroke kick, but once you get it right you will retain the skill.

The kick explained here is the newer style of breaststroke kick. The older version that was still taught back in the 1970s and 1980s was more closely modelled on a real frog kick and involved the legs flexing sideways. It is rarely taught now and in my opinion is more difficult to accomplish anyway. So if you learnt breaststroke kick a long time ago these instructions may seem a little bit different to what you remember.

To kick correctly in breaststroke your feet need to start together with your legs straight. Next bend your knees so your heels go up towards your bottom with your toes pointing upwards. Then turn your toes so they face outwards (towards the pool walls). Finally, whip your legs around until the feet touch again. Your feet should pause for about two seconds at the end of the kick (the glide).

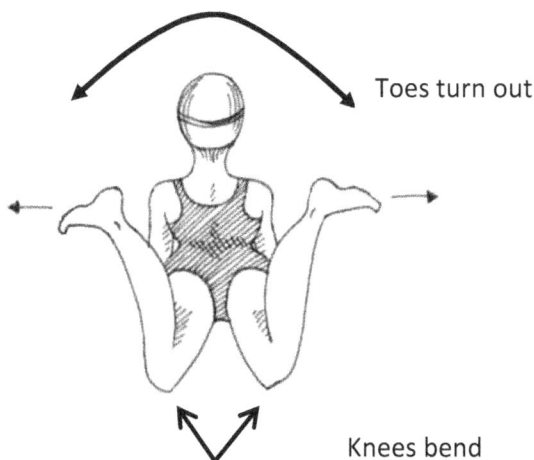

Toes turn out

Knees bend

Practice the kick holding onto the edge of the pool or with your arms draped over the top of a kickboard or with a noodle under your arms (so your head remains out of the water).

If only one of your feet is turning out, position yourself alongside the pool wall (on the side that your foot is not turning out correctly). Kick slowly making sure that your toes touch the wall on each kick. This will force you to think about your foot position.

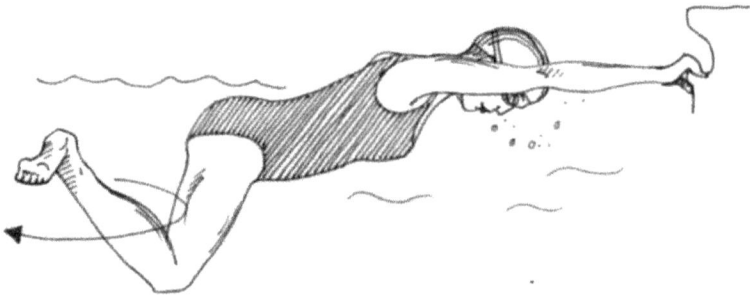

Hold onto the side to practice the kick.

Be patient, as it can take a bit of practice to break your old habit and get the kick right. You can also practice the kick on dry land. Lie on a bed or couch or the floor in a place you can see yourself in a mirror. Watch your feet as they come up – are the toes pointed up and then out?

Another helpful way to correct an incorrect kick is to practice on your back. Use a kickboard or noodle for support and use the same principles but in reverse. Concentrate on both feet pointing to the walls and whipping them around and back together.

THE STROKE

When you have your kick sorted out, you can start on your arm stroke. Again, many adults assume they are doing the breaststroke stroke correctly, when in fact they are not. Begin with your arms fully extended in front of you. Then sweep them out (with palms facing outwards) to make a V position. Next you need to bend your arms at the elbow, dropping your forearms down until they are in the 'scarecrow' position. Finally you need to sweep your arms around in a circular motion and shoot them forward until they are fully extended again.

The only time your arms should pause in the stroke, is when they are at the start and the finish. A common error is to pause them at your side halfway through the stroke. This is generally compounded by pulling the arms too far back., which, by default, pauses the stroke. The key point about breaststroke arms is that everything happens out in front, at no time do your arms pull down by your side.

TIMING

Finally you will need to work on the timing. Unlike freestyle and backstroke your stroke and kick are not performed simultaneously in breaststroke. The stroke comes first, then the kick, with each element providing forward propulsion. If the stroke and kick are done in unison you are effectively halving your forward propulsion, resulting in a much slower stroke.

Push off in streamline position with eyes in the water then begin the stroke. When the hands move apart is when you lift your head up to breathe. When the arms mover out to the V is when you begin your kick. Your stroke should be ahead of your kick and your hands should stay together until your feet touch at the end – that is the signal to begin your next stroke.

You can think of breaststroke in four steps – stroke, breathe, kick and glide (the end of the kick). To get the timing right, focus first on when your head lifts. If it is coming up any later than the moment your hands move apart, the timing for the whole stroke will be out. One common reason people breathe too late in breaststroke is because they are too far under the water. So, naturally if you are further down it will take you longer to surface and breathe. Like freestyle, your front of your head should be just under the surface of the water (ears down). If it is any further down than that, chances are your hips and legs are too low. Remember the heads, hands, hips, heels at the surface of the water rule.

Start your kick when the arms sweep out.

Getting breaststroke correct can take a lot of effort. If you feel your stroke needs a lot of work, I recommend studying instructional videos (check out the links on the website) or perhaps even having one or two stroke correction lessons, if you can manage it. On the other hand, if your breaststroke propels you through the water at a reasonable pace and you are not interested in becoming the next Master's champion, you don't need to get too caught up in getting the technique perfect. Again, think about why you are swimming and what your own personal goals are. I would recommend getting the kick correct at least, but don't get too caught up in the timing if you can't get it exactly right. Remember too that you need to swim a lot of breaststroke at a fairly fast pace to get the same fitness benefit as you would from freestyle.

There is a video available for breaststroke on the website links page.

TUMBLE TURNS AND DIVING

Unless you are planning on competing, the average recreational swimmer doesn't really need to worry too much about tumble turns and diving. Push starts from the wall are perfectly adequate at this level. However, there is no reason you can't work on both these skills if you so desire and I have outlined the basics below.

TUMBLE TURNS

There is no doubt about it a well-executed tumble turn looks fantastic. They are also a great way to build momentum in your swimming and increase the distance you swim. They are a little bit tricky to learn, but like any aspect of swimming, with lots of practice you should be able to master this skill.

A tumble turn is a little bit more involved than a simple somersault under the water. You need to swim close to the wall (about one arm's length away), drop both arms to your side, do half a forward somersault, use your legs to push off the wall on your back while extending your arms in streamline position, then roll back face down and continue swimming! The main mistakes people make are starting the somersault too far from the wall and attempting to roll face down before pushing off. Remember, too, that you need to hold your breath for several seconds when doing a tumble turn. If you use your time at the end of each lap to get a good breath in, you may struggle if you change to tumble turns.

To get a tumble turn right break it into steps – first practice a basic somersault, then practice swimming a few strokes and going straight into a somersault, then practice dropping your arms to your side and doing a somersault, then move to the pool wall and go from a standing position (making sure you push off on your back with arms extended). You actually need to be very close to the wall to do a proper tumble turn. Your legs need to be bent as you flip over so you can get a good push off the wall. It simply doesn't work if you are too far out as you will lose any momentum if you have to stretch your legs out to make contact with the wall. Experiment from a standing position and note how far out you need to be. When you can confidently judge the distance, you need to be from the wall, start swimming a few strokes and practice slowly until you can get all the elements together.

Once you can do a tumble turn in isolation, start working them into your workout. Maybe start at just the deep end only first, then progress to both ends as you improve. During warm up or warm down is a great time to practice, as you will generally be swimming in a more relaxed way. The main challenge when working a tumble turn in, is to control your breathing. Make sure you get a breath just before going into the turn and start exhaling through your nose as you go into the turn (see note 1 below). Although this will be difficult initially, over time you will become much better at it once you get used to not having a big inhale at the end of each lap. Persist through the early attempts that will feel awkward and clunky and you will eventually get to a place where you can do a tumble turn effortlessly.

Tip 1 – Make sure you exhale through your nose as you flip over, otherwise the laws of physics will take over and you will get water up your nose. Not the end of the world, but not fun either. You will probably only make this mistake once or twice!

Tip 2 – If you find it takes too long to roll back over to your front once you push off the wall, experiment with pushing off side on. All it takes is a slight body adjustment once you have flipped, rather than going to your back to push off, plant your feet sideways on the wall and push off that way.

Tip 3 – If you want to speed up your tumble turn ability, practice 20 or 30 at a time. Always include the swim up/swim away – you should aim for a minimum of ten metres – and just keep punching them out until they start feeling better. This is probably easier in shallower water so you can start with your feet on the bottom and get reasonable momentum for your swim in.

I have included a video of tumble turns on the website links.

DIVING

If you have never dived before or it has been a long time since you attempted to dive, please take it slowly. Diving has the potential to cause serious injury at any age, but more so the older (and less flexible) your body is. The main thing to remember is that you need to protect your neck and keep it in a stable position. The only way you can do this is to keep your arms fully extended, pressing against your ears with your hands flat and one top of each other (as you do in streamline position).

When you dive into the water ideally your body should enter through the same small space. Imagine a ring in the water – first your hands, then your shoulders, head, torso, hips, legs and feet should all follow each other through. You have to keep your eyes looking down the whole time. Start with one knee and one foot on the pool edge, then work your way up to standing with bent knees on the pool edge. Do not use the blocks unless you are completely confident in your diving ability. You should also never dive into the shallow end unless you have had some training.

I have included a video of diving on the website links.

OCEAN AND OPEN WATER SWIMMING

This book has concentrated solely on improving your skills in a swimming pool. The main reason for this is that building your swimming skills is much easier in a controlled environment where the water is clear and calm, there are no hidden hazards and you can measure and regulate the distance you swim. If you are interested in ocean or open water swimming, including triathlon or ironman events, it is essential to build up your skills in the pool first and then transition when you are fitter and more confident. You will also need to continue training in the pool to keep your skills and fitness at optimum level. If you really prefer swimming in saltwater and are lucky enough to live in an area that has an ocean pool (a pool that is filled with sea water), you could train there. Bondi Icebergs in Sydney is an example of one of the best ocean pools in the world.

If you decide to give open water swimming a go, there are a few things to remember. While the strokes will be the same, open water swimming is very different to being in a pool. The first thing to be conscious of is safety. Only swim at patrolled beaches or at the very least have a buddy with you. No matter how good a swimmer you believe you are, it is never smart to be out in the open water alone. Don't attempt to ocean swim at beaches that are known to be dangerous. The next thing to consider is individual beach conditions. Depending on whether the tide is high or low there can be exposed rocks and deep gutters/holes that can alter the water depth significantly in a matter of centimetres. You will also need to check for rips. At patrolled beaches read the information board on the sand and/or check with the lifeguards/lifesavers.

When entering the ocean, the first thing you will need to do is navigate the wave zone. This is generally the most challenging part of the swim as you need to expend a fair amount of energy to get through the waves. Wade out until about thigh deep, then move through the waves by diving underneath them using a technique called a 'dolphin dive'. It is basically a shallow dive (with your arms in the streamline position ie at full extension and firm against your ears). Your aim is to grab hold of the sand on the bottom, then draw your legs underneath you and use your feet to push off the bottom and back to the surface. You should push up at a 45 degree angle rather than straight up. The reason to dolphin dive is because it will prevent the waves pushing you back. The closer you are to the bottom, the less you will be impacted by the wave action. Depending on conditions, you can swim between each wave, or you may need to dolphin dive continuously until you clear the wave zone. To get a good visual google dolphin diving or porpoising, there are many videos of ocean swimmers demonstrating this skill.

Once beyond the breaking waves, it is easier to swim continuously. However, depending on the swell, you will probably find yourself moved up and down a lot. It is more difficult to look at the bottom and you can easily get a mouthful of water if you turn to breathe on the wrong side or at the wrong time. To keep track of where you are going, you will need to lift your head forward every so often and make sure you are on track (it is very easy to be moved a substantial distance by an ocean sweep without being aware of it). This technique is called sighting. To keep track of your position, find a fixed object on shore and regularly check your proximity to it. Google 'sighting in ocean swimming' to get some good demo videos.

Open water swimming is definitely more challenging than pool swimming. You need to expend more energy to navigate waves and current and you need to have an awareness of rips, currents and general beach safety. If you are really interested in open water swimming, I suggest you research it further before taking the plunge. I love ocean swimming and recommend it as an amazing way to stay fit and enjoy swimming in a whole new way. However, you do need to be prepared for the different challenges it brings. Like pool swimming, it is something you can train for and become more proficient at.

A great way to improve your open water skills in a safe way is to join an ocean swimming group. Search online for ocean swimming groups in your area. You may be surprised how many of them exist. There are also many training courses available that will teach you ocean swimming skills. Some of these are a few hours, others span over several weeks. Surf clubs will often run ocean skills clinics as well. Again, an online search will point you to such courses in your area. Many companies do travelling clinics as well, which also offer an opportunity to take part.

Apart from triathlon and ironman events, there are many open water swimming events each year with varying distances for beginners to elite. It is a sport that is growing hugely in popularity. Like all organised sporting events, there is a real camaraderie and community of likeminded athletes at open water swims. These events are generally run by Surf Life-Saving Clubs or other similar organisations and, in my experience, most of them are well run with an emphasis on safety and participation. If you are new to ocean swimming, finding an event to train for can be a major incentive. Start with a shorter distance, even if you are a strong pool swimmer. 1.5 – 2 km is ideal. This will allow you to get the feel of an ocean swim event and be challenged but not push yourself too far. Of course, ocean swimming events can be influenced by the weather and surf conditions. Organisers will almost always err on the side of caution if the event is likely to pose risk for the majority or swimmers. All things being fair on the day, you will be organised into a category depending on age/ability. Most events have categories for more competitive swimmers, as well as a "social" category for those who just want to have a go. You will be given a coloured cap to wear and often an electronic timer to wear on your ankle as well. There will be "water safety" people in the water as well, generally on surf lifesaving rescue boards. There will also be Inflatable Rescue Boats (IRBs) in the vicinity. If at any time you feel tired, unwell, uneasy or just unable to continue, raise your hand and somebody will come and help you.

Once in the water you will have a set course to follow. The course is marked by large buoys that are easily visible as you swim. They will often be different colours for different sections. Take the time at the start to visually check the course and understand the direction it is going in. (There will generally be a map on display as well as the organisers verbally explaining the course). Depending on the direction you are travelling, you will either have to keep the marker buoys to your left or your right. If in doubt during the swim, stop for a moment and have a look around. If there are water safety people in the vicinity, ask them. Otherwise just follow the other swimmers (and hope they are going the right way!).

In my experience people either love or hate their first ocean swim, with the majority loving it and becoming addicted to the sport. One of the reasons is because it is a very inclusive sport with events for swimmers of all levels. If your first experience is not a great one, don't give up just yet. Try another event maybe with an easier course or warmer water. Attempt a shorter distance or go in the social wave rather than the competitive one. If you are a triathlete, regular ocean swimming is vital to keep your skills sharp for events. Ocean swim events can be an ideal training opportunity for triathletes without the pressure of your other legs to consider.

CLINICS AND CAMPS

Attending a clinic or a camp can be an amazing opportunity to improve your swimming skills over a short space of time. Generally, they involve filming of your swimming stroke both above and underneath the water and a discussion with a coach while viewing your video. Depending then on the length of the clinic/camp, you will be given specific drills etc to work on.

While they may seem expensive, taking into account the individual coaching attention delivered and the benefits gained, clinics/camps can definitely be seen as a worthwhile investment. Of course a clinic will be shorter, (generally a few hours or a day), while a camp will allow you the opportunity to focus on nothing but your swimming stroke for a week or so, with a group of like-minded people. Given that these camps are usually held in exotic locations around the world, a swim camp can be the ultimate holiday with a purpose.

If you only have the time/money for a clinic, you will have to be a little more disciplined and work on suggested stroke changes yourself in your regular training routine. This is not too difficult, though. Once you have viewed footage of the way you swim, you have a much greater understanding of what you need to change. Clinics sometimes offer the ongoing support and feedback of the coach for an extended period afterwards. An internet search will help you find clinics and camps in your part of the world.

SUGGESTED TRAINING PROGRAMS

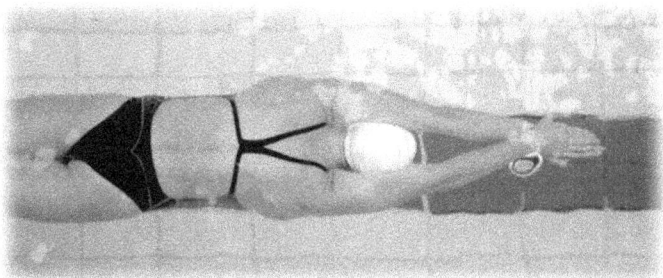

★ Beginner

★ Intermediate

★ Advanced

PREPARING

If you have not swum for a long time (or done any kind of exercise), make sure you have a check-up with your doctor to rule out any problems. If you do have some issues, discuss with your doctor or other health care professional if swimming is advisable and if so take note of any modifications you will need to make. Before you start a swimming session, do some mild stretches of your arms and legs. Although swimming can be a gentle activity, there is still the potential for muscle strains and other sport injuries if you don't prepare your body properly.

ENGAGING YOUR CORE

For those of you who have done Pilates or yoga you will be familiar with 'engaging your core'. All it means is that you should draw your belly button upwards and hold it firm while you swim. This will ensure you use your large core muscles to keep your body in position. If you don't do this, you may find your lower back begins to ache as you get fatigued (and your back sags). For more specific exercises, research core strength – there is a huge amount of information out there.

EASE BACK

If you miss several sessions in a row, it can be difficult to pick up exactly where you left off. Don't be too hard on yourself. Go back a level for the first couple of sessions and work your way back up. The good news is it doesn't take too long to work your way back up. And you will never go right back to where you started (unless you leave it for years between sessions!)

TRAINING DIARY

It is not essential to keep a training diary, but it can be a very helpful tool to assist you with your fitness goals. You can buy training diaries which are set up specifically to record all kinds of information, or you can create your own version. A simple exercise book or spiral note book can do the job just as well. Or if you like technology you can keep notes on your phone, iPod or iPad/tablet (there are also many apps that serve a similar purpose). You can record as much or as little info as you like – but the usual kinds of things to make note of would be the length of your training session, the distance covered, your sprint times and distance times. You can also make note of any injuries or other problems you may be experiencing. If nothing else it is a good way to keep yourself motivated as it details how far you have come.

DO I NEED A TRAINING WATCH?

It seems like everybody has a training watch these days, be it Garmin, TomTom, Fitbit or any other different brands. While these watches are amazing in what they can do and the information they can provide, they are really not necessary to become a better swimmer. You can keep track of how far you have swum by counting your laps. You can work out how many calories you have burned by consulting a chart. The heart rate monitors generally don't work as well underwater but if you really want to test your heart rate you can take your pulse manually. A normal, old-fashioned stopwatch can time your sprints if you don't want to use the pace clock. If you already have one, by all means use it, but don't feel like you need one to become a better swimmer.

JOINING A SQUAD

Many people baulk at the thought of joining a swimming squad. To an outside observer watching swimmers being put through their paces and the sight of a coach with a stopwatch can be a scary thing. And if you are an elite swimmer training for big events, squad sessions probably are to be feared. For adults, however, aiming to improve their fitness and maybe training for a triathlon or similar, squad can be a very beneficial activity.

Most adult squads will be divided into categories, for example Beginner, Intermediate, Advanced, Tri Squad, Mum's Squad or Social Squad. Each pool is different, but you get the idea. The key is choosing the correct fit for yourself. If you are nervous about what a squad might be like, join a social or beginner group to start with and see how you go. If you are comfortably completing the sessions, maybe consider moving to a more difficult squad.

Having a coach making up the session and guiding you through them is far more motivating than having to grind out the laps yourself. They can also push you when required (or not if you don't want to be). They also provide stroke correction when required. Even having a coach to discuss goals with can get you from vaguely considering an event to committing to give it a go.

The other great thing about joining a squad is the social aspect. Having a group of people who enjoy doing the same thing you do is great. Having a chat before and after is also nice. It might even extend to closer friendships outside the pool. It is also fun to have some friendly rivalry and banter amongst the group, making the whole pool experience more enjoyable.

TRAINING SESSIONS

As like the rest of this guide, I have used the word 'relaxed' rather than 'slow' to describe easy, comfortable swimming in the following sessions. Think of relaxed like a gentle stroll rather than a power walk. The word slow often conjures up doings something at a painstaking pace. While this can be helpful for some physical activities, swimming does require a certain rhythm to keep moving, especially in regard to buoyancy. Trying too hard to swim slowly can actually be counterproductive. Relaxed means it is easy and comfortable, not mechanical and clunky. As you become a better swimmer you will soon be able to adjust the pace you swim at and will find where relaxed is versus moderate and fast.

The use of fins/flippers for warm up and warm down is a great idea when doing a swimming session. They allow you to ease into the session and warm up your muscles without fatiguing early. They also allow you to finish your session when you may be feeling tired and might otherwise take an early mark. Warm up in particular is a great time to continue to cement those core skills you worked so hard on, especially breathing and body position. You cannot use fins/flippers for breaststroke as the mechanics of the kick do not work with them on. You can, instead, do butterfly kick if you know how with breaststroke arms. Also referred to as dolphin kick, it involves both legs moving up and down together. Google it if you are interested, otherwise leave the fins off for any breaststroke.

You will be the best judge of which level to start at and when to move up. When you can complete the session easily it is definitely time to move on to harder sets. Conversely if you find the set is too difficult, choose an easier one for the time being and work your way back up.

I have used standard distances of 50/100/200/400/800 metres, but these can be adjusted when swimming in nonstandard pools. Just round up or down relevant to the length of your pool. It is best to swim in a pool at least 25 metres/yards as anything shorter than that doesn't let you build the same distance fitness. In a ten metre pool, for example, you would push off the wall nine times to swim 100 metres as compared to four times in a 25 metre pool or just two times in a 50 metre pool. The more times you push off the wall, the less strokes you will do. Of course if you have no other option, any length will be beneficial, however if you are able to swim at least some of your session in a longer pool your results will be better.

If you want a more comprehensive training plan to get you started, check out the Couch to 1k plan at Get Swimming - www.getswimming.com.au/agtbsc21k. This eight-week graduated plan has 24 sessions that gradually build from 200m up to a full 1km session. As an Adults Guide To Better Swimming Reader you are able to purchase the program at the special discounted price of $9.95. Just copy the link above or scan the QR code below for this offer.

Get Swimming also has ten pack sessions for 1km, 1.5km, 2km and 2.5km distances. As an Adults Guide To Better Swimming reader you can purchase these programs at the discounted price of $5.95. Copy the link (www.getswimming.com.au/10pagtbs) or scan the QR code below.

Couch To 1K

10 Pack Sessions

Beginner Sessions

These early sessions are designed for the beginner who is just starting out. At this level your challenge is to always finish each lap no matter how fatigued you are.

- ✪ Three different sessions

- ✪ Distance is 600 metres or 656 yards

- ✪ Time required is 20 – 30 minutes

- ✪ Equipment needed is kickboard and pull buoy (ankle band if possible) and access to a pace clock or stopwatch

EARLY SESSION #1

Warm Up (fins optional)

- 100 metres easy freestyle with a 30 second rest between laps

- 50 metres of kick on the kickboard

Main Session

- 4 x 50 metres alternating between freestyle and breaststroke (30 second rest between laps)

- 2 x 25 metres freestyle sprint. Swim as fast as you can for this distance. Have a two minute rest between the two sprints. If you are in a 50 metre pool, just swim half way.

- 2 x 50 metres freestyle using a pull buoy (30 second rest between laps). When using the pull buoy really concentrate on your breathing and long strokes.

Swim Down

- 50 metres of easy freestyle or breaststroke

EARLY SESSION #2

Warm Up (fins optional for freestyle)

- 50m freestyle and 50 metres breaststroke with a 20 second rest between laps

- 50 metres breaststroke kick on the kickboard

Main Session

- 2 x 50 metres freestyle Drill #2 (Check back to the drill section)

- 8 x 25 metres freestyle (10 second rest between laps)

- 1 x 50 metres backstroke

- 2 x 25 metres freestyle sprint. Swim as fast as you can for this distance. Have a two minute rest between the two sprints. If you are in a 50 metre pool, just swim half way.

Swim Down

- 50 metres of easy breaststroke

EARLY SESSION #3

Warm Up (fins optional)

- 100 metres relaxed freestyle with a 30 second rest between laps

- 50 metres back kick (either with or without kickboard)

Main Session

- 2 x 50 metres freestyle Drill #1 (Check back to the drill section)

- 2 x 100 metres freestyle with no break between laps. It doesn't matter how slow you go, just keep moving for the whole distance. (1 min break between the two 100m).

- 1 x 50 metres freestyle sprint. Swim as fast as you can for this distance – remember kick faster and increase your stroke rate.

- 1 x 50 metres freestyle using a band only (30 second rest between laps). This can be difficult but it will help you determine if your body position is OK.

Swim Down

- 50 metres of easy backstroke

INTERMEDIATE SESSIONS

These intermediate sessions are designed for the person who has been swimming for several weeks. At the intermediate stage your aim is to eliminate the rest between laps when swimming 100/200 metres and also to decrease your sprint time by at least 1 second each session.

- ✪ Three different sessions

- ✪ Distance is 1 kilometre or 1093 yards

- ✪ Time required is 40 – 50 minutes

- ✪ Equipment needed is kickboard, pull buoy, ankle band, flippers/fins and access to a pace clock or stopwatch

Intermediate Session #1

Warm Up (fins optional for freestyle)

- 200 metres freestyle with pull buoy (5 second rest between laps if you need it)

- 100 metres kick on kickboard (either freestyle or breaststroke kick or both)

Main Session

- 1 x 50 metre freestyle sprint (aiming for under 1 min 5 sec)

- 2 x 25 metre freestyle sprint (aiming for under 35 sec)

- 100 metres easy breaststroke (5 second rest if needed between laps)

- 100 metres backstroke (no rest between laps)

- 200 metres freestyle (aim for no rest between laps or 5 sec if you need it)

Swim Down

- 200 metres freestyle with flippers

INTERMEDIATE SESSION #2

Warm Up

- 300 metres freestyle with flippers or pull buoy (continuous)

Main Session

- 2 x 50 metres freestyle sprint (aiming for under 1 min 5 sec each time). One min rest between sprints.

- 4 x 50 metres Drill #3

- 200 metres freestyle (aim for no rest between laps or 5 sec if you need it)

Swim Down

- 200 metres alternating between the three strokes each 25 metres – eg 25 m freestyle, 25 m breaststroke, 25 m backstroke then repeat.

Intermediate Session #3

Warm Up

- 200 metres freestyle with pull buoy (aim for no rest between laps or 5 sec between 100m if you need it)

- 150 metres kick on kickboard (alternate freestyle and breaststroke)

Main Session

- 4 x 25 metre freestyle sprint (aiming for under 35 sec)

- 200 metres freestyle (no rest between laps)

- 2 x 50 metres band only freestyle (concentrate on correct body position)

- 150 metres freestyle (no rest between laps if possible)

Swim Down (fins optional)

- 100 metres relaxed backstroke

ADVANCED SESSIONS

These advanced sessions are designed for the person who has been swimming for six weeks or more. At this stage you should be comfortable swimming distances of 200/400/800 metres continuously and should have fairly short rest periods between sets.

- ✪ Three different sessions

- ✪ Distance is 2 kilometres or 1 mile 427 yards

- ✪ Time required is 60 – 70 minutes

- ✪ Equipment needed is kickboard, pull buoy, ankle band, flippers/fins and access to a pace clock or stopwatch

ADVANCED SESSION #1

Warm Up (fins optional)

- 200 metres freestyle

- 200 metres kick on kickboard

- 200 metres freestyle with pull buoy

- 2 x 50 metres (25 metres kick in streamline position then 25 metres normal freestyle)

Main Session

- 8 x 50 metres on variable pace (this means first 50m is half hard/half easy, second 50m is half easy/half hard, third 50m is all easy and the fourth 50m is a sprint at full pace). Have one minute rest between the 2 x 200 metres).

- 1 x 100 metre freestyle sprint (aiming for approximately double your 50 metre sprint time)

- 1 x 400 metres at a moderate pace

- 1 x 200 metres alternating breaststroke and backstroke

Swim Down (fins optional)

- 200 metres choice stroke(s) at easy pace

ADVANCED SESSION #2

Warm Up (fins optional)

- 100 metres freestyle kick

- 1 x 200 metres alternating breaststroke and backstroke

- 1 x 200 metres single arm freestyle with flippers, alternating arms each lap. 10 sec rest between laps.

Main Session

- 6 x 50 metres band only freestyle (10 sec between laps)

- 400 metres freestyle max effort (aiming for 9 minutes or under)

- 2 x 200 metre freestyle 100 easy/100 fast

- 4 x 100 metres freestyle building from easy to fast with each 100

Swim Down (fins optional)

- 200 metres choice stroke(s) at an easy pace

ADVANCED SESSION #3

Warm Up (fins optional for freestyle/backstroke)

- 200 metres freestyle

- 200 metres backstroke

- 100 metres breaststroke kick on kickboard

Main Session

- 1 x 800 metres freestyle continuous. Swim at a moderate pace and concentrate on long strokes and relaxed breathing. This should feel comfortable.

- 8 x 25 metres freestyle sprint on 45 seconds. This means you do you sprint and rest until 45 seconds is up then go again. If you are looking at the pace clock you would start on the 60, then 45, then 30, then 15, then 60 again. The faster you swim the more rest you get.

- 3 x 100 metres freestyle with a 15 sec rest between each set

Swim Down

- 200 metres alternating breaststroke/backstroke

IN CONCLUSION

I hope Adults Guide To Better Swimming has been a helpful guide that has inspired and motivated you to really work on your swimming skills. If you did enjoy the book, I would really appreciate if you could leave a rating and review on Amazon as that helps other readers find my book too.

As mentioned earlier, I have included some links to YouTube videos for particular skills. Should you wish to view them on the website, you can find them at: https://theswimguide.weebly.com/links

I genuinely hope that you do stick at improving your swimming skills. It is a sport that I love – both as a teacher and a participant. In my opinion there is no better place to be than in the water on a summer's morning and the 'feel good' effect carries on all day. Without question the days I swim in the morning I have much more energy and mental clarity. But don't take my word for it – have a go for yourself and see what I'm talking about.

About The Author

I am a lifelong lover of swimming! Right from my first introduction to the water I couldn't get enough of it. In saying that, though, I was very much a self-taught swimmer. Although my school did have a swimming program, it was much more basic than the ones offered today. There was only so much one teacher could do when faced with 30 kids of varying ability in one big group!

It wasn't until I was at university that I attended my first stroke correction class and realised that I could progress up to squad level – I just had to work on my basics first. I was pretty gung-ho and swam every day for about six weeks, during which time I improved massively. It still took about three months, however, to match the skill of the others in the squad.

Working in a stressful full-time job, I often thought about being a swimming teacher. I knew it wasn't a full-time option, but when the opportunity came for me to reduce my work hours, I did my teacher training and started teaching swimming one day per week. I love it and being a Learn To Swim teacher is the perfect anti-dote to the other stresses in my life.

As for my own swimming – you will still find me at squad at 5.15 most mornings on the beautiful Gold Coast in Queensland. I love to take the newbies under my wing and get them through those difficult first few sessions and share in their joy when they start making big leaps towards great technique and fitness.

If you have any further questions please email me at:
katieswimguides@yahoo.com.au

Happy Swimming!

Katie Smith

CONTACT INFORMATION

If you wish to get in touch you can email:
katieswimguides@yahoo.com.au

You may also wish to check out the **Get Swimming** website, which has more resources and information. www.getswimming.com.au

www.ingramcontent.com/pod-product-compliance
Lightning Source LLC
Chambersburg PA
CBHW022123280326
41933CB00007B/522